Regan,

RU SigEp...
what more can you say?
Thanks for being a
great brother. I
hope you enjoy the
book and wish you
continued success on
your leadership journey!

EZ

Published by EDGE Publishing Company
Manassas, VA
www.edgepublishingcompany.com

YOUR LEADERSHIP MAP:

Navigating Your Way
to
Greater Organizational
Efficiency, Effectiveness, and Success

Ed Zimmerman

EDGE Publishing Company
Manassas, VA
www.edgepublishingcompany.com

Cover design by Sadie E. Nezich of Concord Consulting, LLC
Editing and formatting by Amanda E. Clark of Grammar Chic, Inc. - www.grammarchic.net

ISBN 978-1-4507-5109-4

Published by EDGE Publishing Company
8939 Sweetbriar St.
Manassas, VA 20110
(703)447-3780
www.edgepublishingcompany.com

Acknowledgments

I want to thank my guest experts: Jim McCarthy, Mike Mathes, Pete Paradise, Jeff Pottinger, Fran Trentley, and Tom Corley, for their contribution to this book. Sharing their thoughts and experiences makes the book much more insightful. I also want to thank Carla Nixon, Michael Young, Lynnette Anderson, and Abigail O'Neill for helping me further develop and communicate concepts within the book. Likewise, Kevin Quirk, Sadie Nezich, Amanda Clark, and Phil Vera were instrumental in taking the book through the final editing and publishing process.

Lastly, I want to thank Caroline, Rob, and Rachel for being the supportive family willing to make the sacrifices required for me to pursue my professional dreams.

Table of Contents

Introduction 1

Chapter 1: Plotting the Journey to Success. 7

Chapter 2: Leadership Map Principles - Empower Your Team 19

Chapter 3: People - It All Starts With People. 31

Chapter 4: Process - Finding the Right Balance. 69

Chapter 5: Technology - The Great Enabler. 89

Chapter 6: Strategic Planning - Yes, You Need It!. 115

Chapter 7: Relationships - The Key Ingredient to Enabling Success. . 139

Chapter 8: Opportunity - Yours Could Be Right in Front of You. 159

Chapter 9: Are You Ready to Take the Next Step?. 175

Acronyms 178

Appendix 1: LM Azimuth Check Assessment Form 179

Introduction

As you will quickly see, *YOUR LEADERSHIP MAP: Navigating Your Way to Greater Organizational Efficiency, Effectiveness, and Success* introduces simple principles that can be applied to any leadership situation. These principles are similar to those of navigating from point A to point B on a planned trip. To successfully complete your journey you require navigational skills and tools. Leading an organization is no different. The key to a successful organizational journey is to be properly equipped and prepared to move when and where required, based on knowledge of the situation. A map is a key component that enables you to plan your trip and a "Leadership Map" (LM) is a key element in leading your organization to success. Why provide a map for leading organizations? Whether you're a seasoned leader/manager with a wealth of personal experience to draw from in your daily decisions and relationships or a new leader/manager in the process of defining your professional values and what works for you—or somewhere in between—you can benefit from using the LM to build a strong, organized leadership structure. As I will discuss in this book, the LM is a tool that provides individuals and organizations direction, much like a map or a compass. Your experience or familiarity with a particular situation will dictate how you use the LM. You may refer to the LM often when you are in unfamiliar territory or you may only use it to provide a quick azimuth check (glancing at your compass) when on familiar ground to ensure you are heading in the right direction.

It may sound funny, but I am truly passionate about organizational dynamics, and the way leaders/managers contribute to those dynamics has fascinated me since my college days at Radford University in southern Virginia. I was exposed to leadership, as a more formal subject, during my involvement with Radford's Army ROTC program. This happens to be the same timeframe during which I was exposed to land navigation and map reading. This could be one reason I was quick to see the similarities in the two subjects. Both can be broken down into essential principles that allow you to deal with different situations (or territories) in similar but unique manners. A map provides important information for land navigation but sometimes the situation on the ground is different than the map and you must be prepared to navigate through those situations using a compass to check your azimuth and keep you going in the right direction. Similarly, information is critical for a leader to make good decisions but he must be able to adapt to changes based on the situation.

I could talk longer about these similarities but I want to get to what this book is really all about— leadership. I use subtle references to navigation only to help communicate different aspects of leading or managing. Leading an organization can sometimes become a very complex and complicated endeavor. My experience has enabled me to recognize the dynamics involved in leading people, as well as the importance of being able to effectively communicate with those people. With that in mind, I have tried to make this book as straightforward as possible. The key to successfully communicating any subject is to make the complex aspects of the topic simple. It is hard for me to imagine that anyone reading this book has not had to plan and execute a trip from one location to another. Using a simple theme related to navigation helps to level the playing field for leaders who may be at different levels of experience and education.

For more than a quarter century, my fascination with leadership has evolved and I have become more knowledgeable and aware of the skills required to lead and manage. These skills are separate from each other yet interdependent. The fact is that we all possess leadership and management skills and use these skills daily to meet our objectives. However, most people spend very little time gaining an appreciation of the subject or improving either their leadership or management skills. Your success in life will ultimately come down to your ability to influence other people who in some way impact your life. To successfully influence others in any type of sustained manner is dependent on your ability to lead. This book and the LM offer unique ways of looking at the principles and best practices I've learned through more than 25 years of organizational leadership in both military and civilian roles. Some of the ideas will be familiar to you and some will be new, but the key is the way they all work together to give you a solid basis for your leadership approach.

Let me tell you a little bit more about myself and the life experiences that have shaped my views on leadership before we jump into the chapters of the book. I have more than 25 years of leadership in diverse organizations going back to my college days, where I was a leader in Army ROTC as well as my fraternity. Upon graduating from Radford University in 1985, I entered the Army as a Second Lieutenant. As a Quartermaster Officer I primarily focused on logistics. As my career progressed, I was exposed to many leadership opportunities from an operational and educational perspective. Over time, I became practiced in a wide range of functions that include strategy, policy, operations management, information systems management, logistics, program and acquisition management, lifecycle management, financial management, and human resources management. Through all of my roles, I strived to be an empowering leader and team builder. I believed in being an action-oriented decision-maker, keeping a focus on the strategic vision while developing targeted solutions to problems.

I served for over 20 years as an Officer in the U.S. Army. My diverse leadership experience in elite military organizations, which included Delta Force and the White House Communications Agency, contributed to my success as a leader in many formal and informal roles. In 2006, I founded Zimmerman Consulting LLC. As a result of my consulting business, I have had the opportunity to assist leaders and managers in all types of organizations become more efficient and effective in performing their mission and achieving their vision. I also have been fortunate enough to be exposed to many organizations and have seen how the organizational dynamics related to people, processes, and technology have influenced that organization's success or lack of success. In addition to earning a Bachelor of Science degree in Biology from Radford University, I earned a master's degree with a concentration on organizational change management while I was attending the Army's Command and General Staff College. With my life experience as the foundation, I believe that the only truly successful way to lead is to do so holistically: considering all factors or perspectives. The principles I outline in *YOUR LEADERSHIP MAP: Navigating Your Way to Greater Organizational Efficiency, Effectiveness, and Success* have evolved from the examples of family, friends, coaches, fellow military leaders, and many, many others I've encountered in my life. Ultimately, they all contributed to this LM and my techniques to help an organization navigate to success. I've also been influenced by Stephen Covey (*Seven Habits of Highly Effective People*), Jim Collins (*Good to Great*), and, of course, U.S. Army leadership doctrine. I've devoted a lot of time to studying best practices in

3

process improvement, including International Organization of Standards 20000 for information technology (IT) service management, CMMI (Capability Maturity Model Integration), Lean Six Sigma (LSS), Earned Value Management (EVM), and supply chain management (SCM). I'm also a big believer in Knowledge Management (KM) doctrine, which examines how people, processes, and technology align to create and disseminate knowledge critical to how organizations operate on a daily basis. As a result of my experience, formal and informal education, and life's observations, I have learned that you must break down complex leadership situations into simple basic principles or tenets to keep you and your team focused. I believe the LM does just that.

As you read about the LM, you may find that some elements feel like a perfect fit, while others are a little less relevant to your immediate situation. That's okay— the purpose of the LM is to serve as a guide, providing direction as you develop as a leader/manager so you can better understand your role and those of others in your organization to help you, not to lock you into a single mode of operations. The LM is about looking at proven systematic approaches to bring together people, processes, and technology to reach a common goal: making the organization more efficient and effective, improving performance, and ultimately achieving the organizational vision. The goal is to continually improve— to help organizations and the leaders/managers that drive them to be better tomorrow than they are today.

Throughout the book, I present quotes from great leaders who I think exemplify the element of leadership we're exploring. You may have your own heroes and those who inspire you, and I encourage you to use the book's margins to add in notes, record your reactions to the content, and jot down questions to look at later. You'll also find boxes that highlight key phrases and concepts that I use in discussing the LM and how you can grow as a leader/manager. I also include many of my own experiences, examples drawn from simple, everyday situations in all kinds of organizations, as well as illustrations to represent the LM in action.

At the end of Chapters 3-8, I include reflections from guest experts with whom I have a business and/or personal relationship. Their reflections bring in alternative perspectives that complement the content within that chapter and the overall concept of the LM. Each guest expert brings their life's experience as they answer questions related to how concepts within that chapter have somehow shaped their lives. I think you will find their reflections to be thought provoking and another opportunity for you to reflect on your leadership identity.

In *YOUR LEADERSHIP MAP: Navigating Your Way to Greater Organizational Efficiency, Effectiveness, and Success*, I provide tools that will help you to consistently and effectively evaluate the necessary steps to effect change at all levels of organizational leadership and management. An "azimuth check assessment" is an important tool to keep you on course by continually assessing where you are and where you are going. You'll notice that I may use such terms as organization, team, company, group, association, or even community of practice/interest (COP/COI) as interchangeable terms; all of these represent a collection of people who have a relationship based on a common goal. I also want you to recognize that, despite the type, purpose, or make-up of an organization, I believe that there are far more common traits to all organizations than there are differences. Whether you are coaching a youth sports team or leading a private company, military organization, or a volunteer group, success comes down to your understanding of people, processes, and technology, and your ability to adapt to unique situations.

As a consultant, I am often called in when organizations are in crisis. They waited too long to seek help. Although we can succeed in addressing the crisis and getting the organization on course, like many things in life, it is normally much easier to maintain a level of proficiency than it is to initially establish that level of proficiency. As we begin this journey together, I acknowledge that readers will be turning to this book for different reasons. Your organization may be in crisis, or maybe it is doing well but not attaining the success desired. Maybe your organization is on a good course but, as a leader reading this book, you want to avoid potential potholes or you are seeking new ways to improve. Maybe you just want to become a better leader yourself. Regardless of why you have turned to this book, it is a step in the right direction. You have made the initial effort to become better as a leader and as a team/organization. When I work with individuals who are proactively seeking improvement the results have always been far more impressive than working with individuals who are "participating" in the improvement effort because they "have to." I am always excited to enter into a learning dynamic with an individual or a team that seeks to become more efficient, effective, and successful. I think you will enjoy our experience together and find it personally and professionally rewarding.

My hope is that you will use the LM, in conjunction with your personal experience, to create your own leadership identity. We are all leaders; those who are effective are the ones who recognize their ability to make an impact, and who act on it. Be that leader.

Chapter 1

Plotting the Journey to Success

Nothing is particularly hard if you divide it into small jobs.
- Henry Ford

If you were going to take a long journey, moving yourself and your organization from your current location to another location, simple and effective navigational tools and skills would be required. An organization's journey to becoming better in the future is no different. *YOUR LEADERSHIP MAP: Navigating Your Way to Greater Organizational Efficiency, Effectiveness, and Success* captures in very straightforward terms how to be a successful leader who can navigate an organization through different challenges by staying true to basic principles and characteristics associated with people, processes, and technology. A primary focus of this book is to introduce what I call a Leadership Map (LM), which can help navigate you to organizational efficiency and effectiveness.

My goal with the LM is to empower you, as a leader and manager, to consistently and efficiently look at all actions required to effect desirable changes, within the full spectrum of organizational leadership and management. There are many individuals who do not understand the importance of having a mapped out plan that can guide you to success. A map enables you to plot where you are and where you are going. A map combined with other navigational tools can guide you around obstacles, ultimately allowing you to reach your desired destination. I have developed the LM to simplify how I approach the never-ending journey of organizational leadership. The LM promotes a navigational process that, like a map, can help guide you in your journey to success. As you look at the upcoming LM diagram you will notice that the LM addresses critical characteristics associated with people, processes, and technology. Later in the book, I will cover these characteristics and how to assess yourself and your organization using these characteristics as a guide. You will also notice that the LM is a systematic approach of looking at people, processes, and technology in a manner that can be adapted to any type of organization and situation. This powerful approach to leading creates efficiency and effectiveness throughout all levels of an organization. As you become more familiar with the LM, I hope that you will analyze the challenges that you face in your organizational or communities of practice/communities of interest (COP/COI) interactions, using the LM as a guide. As you go through this book I am confident that you will see how the map can help navigate you and your organization to become more efficient and effective.

Organizational Efficiency and Effectiveness, the Holistic View

You see things; and you say 'Why?' But I dream things that never were and I say 'Why not?' - George Bernard Shaw

Candidly stated, the LM exists to assist leaders/managers in enhancing organizational efficiency and effectiveness. Everything we do should contribute in some fashion to the efficiency or effectiveness of the organization. Change for change's sake is generally not a positive experience. Because achieving efficiency and effectiveness is the primary purpose of the LM it is important that I clearly communicate what I mean by efficient and effective. When you think of efficiency you should think about how you achieve your desired result in the most cost-effective manner possible. Although you can measure efficiency in many ways, such as man hours or time, ultimately you can measure it in dollars: the cost of doing business. How much money does your organization have to pay to produce the desired result?

Think about effectiveness without regard to cost. How valuable is the end result to your customer? Effectiveness can be enhanced when a result is achieved faster or the result performs at a higher level of accuracy or precision. Ultimately, effectiveness is a "better" end result. Normally there is a cost associated with making an end result more effective. Business leaders must determine if the cost is worth the enhanced effectiveness or if some or all of the cost can be passed on to the customer. These are the types of senior leader decisions that make or break a company.

The continuous journey for the leader is to make the organization more efficient and effective over time. The LM and this book are devoted to that never-ending navigational endeavor of becoming a better leader/manager and creating a more efficient and effective organization. Now take a few minutes and study the LM in ***Figure 1*** before I walk through this diagram from top to bottom and left to right. If you look at it now and analyze it you will develop an initial impression that will resonate with you. I further suggest you make a quick copy of this diagram for easy reference as you read through the first few chapters. As you do, the LM will become second nature to you. As you will soon see, this is not complicated, but it is helpful to have an easy reference as you initially get familiar with the map. I refer to this diagram often throughout the entire book and you will enjoy your reading more if you feel intimately familiar with the LM.

Leadership Navigation:
Your Journey to Leadership and Organization Success

Purpose:
Organizational Efficiency and Effectiveness to Achieve Success

Lead and Manage

- Monitor
- Measure
  - Individual
  - Team

Principles

- Communicate
- Guide/Feedback
  - Inspire
  - Empower

Results

People, Processes, and Technology

Team

- Plan
- Execute

Principles:

• People, processes, and technology map to every organizational function	• Continual navigation involving people, processes, and technology leads to improvement	• A direction change in people, processes, or technology requires an azimuth check of the other two

Characteristics:

People	Processes	Technology
• Trust	• Simple and focused	• Enabler
• Passion	• Standardized and repeatable	- To leadership
• Knowledge and skill	• Adaptable	- To management
• Complementary		• Accelerates results
• Empowerment		

Figure 1: Leadership Map

Moving into the LM, immediately below the purpose, there are three circles that represent: (1) the leader/manager, (2) the team of individuals that the leader/manager oversees, and (3) the results circle to the left, which represents the results of the entire team. Your organization exists for a purpose, and the effectiveness of the organization will be judged by the results. The success of the organization is dependent on the relationships and flow of information between people involved in the cyclic interaction within the arrows in the diagram. The leader/manager in the diagram can be one person or a team of people. Each of us has leadership skills and management skills; the key is to use these skills appropriately in our role within an organization. The LM captures how leadership and management skills continually guide an organization. The importance of understanding the relationship between both types of skills, as they relate to the LM, enables you to fully take advantage of the cyclic nature of leading versus managing. Leading without the benefit of management feedback can be viewed in the same fashion as moving in a direction and then suddenly turning 90 degrees or even 180 degrees for no apparent reason. Because a leader or a manager requires skills associated with the other it is common for people to refer to the leaders and managers interchangeably. As I will discuss shortly, managers and leaders really have a different role. Since this book is on leadership, I will primarily focus on the leader and my reference to management will normally be with respect to management skills that a leader also must possess.

All of us are both a leader/manager, as well as a team member within different organizations or under different circumstances. Most everyone has a boss to whom they report, and a team of peers with whom they work in some fashion. These same people normally have leadership responsibilities, based on position or situations. Further, remember that you are a member of many formal and informal groups (organizations) that exist for a common purpose. These groups or organizations can be characterized as communities of practice (COP) or communities of interest (COI) and range from a formal company and/or division within a company to a group of individuals from different companies working together for a common purpose. Examples include a relationship among wholesale, retail, and customer organizational representatives or a military coalition made up of different countries. If you take the time to think about how many COI relationships you have, you may find that you are in anywhere between 10 and 20 groups or organizations at any one time. Start thinking about the relationships you have in your work environment, social settings, and within your family, and the number of COIs can quickly grow. For example, at work you belong to your parent organization and maybe one or two formal subordinate organizations within that parent organization (directorate, division, and/or group). You may be working cross-functionally with other companies or within your company on two to five projects at any one time and also be a part of the company softball team. Now start looking at your personal life and, as you can see, the number of COIs quickly multiply when you look at all your relationships. Because some of these relationships may only exist for a short period of time you can appreciate how dynamic a COI view of relationships can be. We will talk about this in more detail later in the book.

Looking at the LM diagram, you will notice that the process flow is represented by the large arrows. This LM process connects the people involved in producing results and ideally improves those results over time, based on feedback into the system. Technology, which is an enabler for making the improvements within the organization, helps to connect the people who are involved in the specific processes. In the center of the diagram is a compass that represents the principles that are the core of the LM and makes it possible for a leader to navigate the organization. Immediately below the diagram is a box that captures the three principles that represent the core of LM. These three principles acknowledge that people, processes, and technology affect all aspects of an organization and thus must be considered if the organization is to continually move forward. The relationship among people, processes, and technology is very close and a change in one area requires at least a look at the potential changes or effects in the other two areas. You cannot expect to reengineer a process without looking at both the technology involved and the people involved.

Finally, at the bottom of the diagram, there are the three blocks that capture the key characteristics of people, processes, and technology that synergistically support the principles of the LM. Significant to this LM is that you recognize that you lead people, you manage processes, and you use technology to enable your ability to lead and manage. Successfully navigating an organization is all about people, processes, and technology; that's why we'll be talking about it often throughout the book.

People

We've already discussed how individuals use skills associated with leadership and management. The leader must communicate vision, as well as provide guidance and feedback that inspire actions toward a common purpose or mission. The leader must ultimately empower in-

> **All of us are both a leader/manager as well as a team member within different organizations or under different circumstances.**

dividuals to achieve results. When you empower others you create individuals who are far more likely to produce the results needed to succeed. The leader is focused on people and effectiveness.

The manager organizes tasks, obtains things needed to perform the tasks, and monitors the results of the tasks. A manager ensures there are reliable, efficient, and repeatable processes in place. The manager focuses on processes and efficiencies so the organization can perform the mission and achieve the vision that the leader communicated. A key factor to achieving the optimal process is effectively measuring the performance of individuals and teams.

For leaders, managers, and team members there are key characteristics that promote optimal performance. Trust, passion, knowledge and skill, complementing the team, and empowerment to execute are key characteristics of successful people and teams. The first three are primarily focused on individuals and the last two are more focused on the individual's relationship to the team.

Processes

All successful organizations have processes in place to streamline workflow and ensure the mission is accomplished not only effectively but as efficiently as possible. The best organizations have processes for every aspect of the mission, whether operational or administrative in nature. As represented in the LM, processes pertain to leaders communicating to the team, the development of a plan, the execution of the plan, and finally the monitoring of the execution. You also can think of processes as habits for individuals or plays of a sports team. Whether you are talking about processes, individual habits, or plays on a sports team, what you really care about is achieving the desired result, at the least cost; or, in another words, the greatest efficiency. This means that the results must be measured against a benchmark and continually monitored for areas to improve upon.

The process box in the LM (*Figure 1*) captures key characteristics of a successful process. A simple, focused process that accomplishes the intended result in the most efficient way is the goal. The ability to standardize processes, not only for team members within functional areas but across disciplines, is an ideal way to promote efficiency. Repeatedly obtaining the desired results also is essential to process success. Lastly, processes must be adaptable to the inevitable change that you can expect based on such factors as advances in technology and a better understanding of the processes themselves.

Technology

Technology is the great enabler for both leaders and managers. It is through technology that leaders communicate and managers get performance feedback. The use of technology provides more accurate and timely communication and feedback. Newer technology facilitates changes to old processes and creates cost savings through previously unrealized efficiencies. As newer technologies emerge and older technologies evolve, processes can drastically change. Technology is the primary driver for change and we tend to overlook it because it forces us to deal with change on what is almost a constant basis.

Creating a Knowledge-Based Organization

Wisdom is not a product of schooling but of the lifelong attempt to acquire it. - Albert Einstein

An organization that uses the LM to continually improve is soon on its way to becoming what I call a knowledge-based organization (KBO). A KBO is one that recognizes the importance of information and uses this information in ways to become more efficient and effective in performing its daily mission. The LM facilitates an approach to information management

> **A knowledge-based organization is one that recognizes the importance of information and uses this information in ways to become more efficient and effective...**

that provides individuals with the information they need to perform at a higher level. The aggregation and distribution of this information creates an organizational knowledge base that influences continual improvements within all aspects of the organization.

People who can think on their feet and adapt to the ever-changing environment that organizations face today will be key players in building the KBO. In addition to recruiting the right type of people, leaders must create an environment that promotes individual and team learning, an environment that is able to capitalize on knowledge obtained through education and experience. This type of environment promotes expanding the knowledge base of the organization as a whole. This is accomplished by managing information in an open manner that develops people, processes, and technology. Knowledge is obtained by asking questions and seeking the answer.

Using the Map to Promote Growth

We can't solve problems by using the same kind of thinking we used when we created them. - Albert Einstein

Whether your organization is in the private or public sector, a sports team, or volunteer group, they all have a dynamic that is similar in nature and can benefit from the LM. But not all organizations have a solid foundation on which to grow. Consider these questions:

1. Does your organization have a mission and vision?
2. Do you understand your organization's mission and vision? What are they?

3. Do you understand your role in supporting the mission and achieving the vision? Explain.

If you answered yes to all of these questions, then congratulations— you are in a small group of people who understand their role and how it supports the greater purpose of the organization. But now ask yourself these two questions:

1. How confident are you that the rest of the people on your team would answer yes to the first three questions?
2. What is the cost to you, your organization, and your customers if there is a lack of understanding in regard to how each individual is part of the bigger picture?

Let's take a moment to consider what an organization might look like when no one knows the goals and mission. Picture a peewee soccer team with a dozen 6 to 8 year-olds who know only "get the ball" or "stay in position." A mob of kids chase the ball everywhere it goes and even take the ball from their own teammates, while at the same time a handful of others stand in one place waiting for the ball to come right to them before they kick it. It's cute to watch but no way to win a soccer game.

Now think about a soccer team in which the coach has taken the time to communi- | **Whether your organization is in the private or public sector, a sports team, or volunteer group, they all have a dynamic that is similar in nature and can benefit from the LM.**

cate and teach the players the team's mission, and how each individual player supports that mission. Players understand when to go after the ball, based on their position and in support of the larger team strategy. When players understand their role, even young children can help move the ball effectively around the field with the intent of scoring a goal. The coach can visually measure improvement of each individual player, as well as the team as a whole, and provide additional feedback (coaching). The team continually becomes better and realizes the overall vision as they eventually become the best soccer team they can be.

You may be a little old for peewee soccer, but the principles for building a successful team are the same regardless of size and purpose. Whether you are coaching a youth sports team, leading a company in the private sector, or a part of a military organization, success comes down to your understanding of people, processes, and technology and your ability to adjust techniques in each, based on the LM principles and the uniqueness of the situation.

Conclusion

The upcoming chapters highlight the characteristics of people, processes, and technology. I discuss these characteristics in terms that underscore the significance to the principles of meshing people, processes, and technology in a manner that enhances the operational aspects of an organization and is the essence of the LM. Entire books can be, and have been, written on many of these characteristics but our role here is to put them in context with the LM. Before talking about the characteristics of people, processes, and technology you must gain a better appreciation of the three principles that are the essence of the LM.

In the next chapter, we will break down the principles of the LM and analyze how the simple and holistic structure can help you plot your path to leadership success and give you the strategies you need to help your team score. At the end of each chapter we will use a table to capture broad benefits related to leadership/management, as well as to the organization as a whole, based on the key concepts discussed in the chapter. The following table captures broad benefits associated with the LM as discussed in this chapter.

Key concepts and benefits to you as a leader and to the organization

LM provides a simple road map or guide to leading and managing

Benefits to the Leader/Manager:	Benefits to the Organization:
• Adaptive approach to guide you in decision making • Enables you to break down complex issues to root problems • Provides you with a framework to enhance your skills	• Relevant to all functional aspects of any organization • Provides a simple picture so the organization gains common understanding of the situation • Focuses on efficiency (waste reduction) and effectiveness (improved results)

Enhances understanding of interdependent relationship among people, processes, and technology

Benefits to the Leader/Manager:	Benefits to the Organization:
• Provides you flexibility to solve problems in different manners based on circumstances • Easy access to information for better decision making	• Solutions to problems not dependent solely on personnel • Access to information, creating a knowledge-based or learning organization

Chapter 2

Leadership Map Principles -

Empower Your Team

It takes more courage to reveal insecurities than to hide them, more strength to relate to people than to dominate them, more "manhood" to abide by thought-out principles rather than blind reflex. Toughness is in the soul and spirit, not in muscles and an immature mind.
- Alex Karras

The LM principles are three simple statements that are aligned with one purpose: to navigate organizational efficiency and effectiveness to achieve success. The fundamental function of the LM principles is to leverage the fact that every organization is affected by— rooted in, in fact— people, processes, and technology. Before we discuss the three principles in more detail, consider how these three areas influence every activity and improvement initiative you might undertake as a leader/manager, and how this can empower your team, developing stronger leaders and a stronger team.

- People, processes, and technology map to every organizational function: Pick an area within your work environment, a social network or COI. Identify the people, the processes, and the technology involved in a specific aspect of the COI, such as identifying and tracking tasks.
- Continual navigation involving people, processes, and technology leads to improvement: List two or three changes with respect to people, processes, or technology that could possibly improve the function you have identified above.

- A direction change in people, processes, or technology requires an azimuth check of the other two: Take your short list of changes and identify the impact each change could have on the other two areas.

This quick mental drill provides you with a first-hand account of the power of having awareness associated with the interdependencies of people, processes, and technology.

Principle 1: People, Processes, and Technology Map to Every Organizational Function

You only have to do a very few things right in your life so long as you don't do too many things wrong. - Warren Buffett

At the end of the day, every function within an organization is founded on people, processes, and technology. The mental exercise we just completed should help you grasp this first principle; however, consider as an example what was involved when you applied for and was hired within your current organization. You likely talked to key leaders and HR representatives who followed some type of outlined process that was enabled by technology in some fashion to move required information to the appropriate people to facilitate the hiring process. The overall intent of this process is to make sure that the organization is bringing in the right person to do a specific job that will support the overall success of the organization.

Although what makes a business successful may vary from company to company, something that all effective organizations have in common is a strong alignment between organizational functions and the overall mission and vision of the organization. In other words, the things employees do on a day-to-day basis directly support the company's strategic goals and its reason for existence. Sounds obvious, right? But it's not always that simple. We'll get to that part in a moment.

Another thing effective organizations have in common is that each team and every individual on a team has responsibilities tied to a purpose and goal(s) that match up with the company mission. Ideally, individuals and teams should also understand how they fit into the bigger picture and how their actions affect the organization's ultimate success in both small and large ways.

Third, every task performed by a team or individual should be supported by an efficient process and associated technologies that enable task completion. Technology can include anything from a million-dollar computer system to a pencil and paper. For the purposes of this discussion, anything outside the human body is technology.

As I said, it's not always that simple. Less efficient organizations also have people, processes, and technology involved in every function of the organization, but often at varying degrees of recognition. Often, organizations are not exactly clear about what their goals are. It's all too common for subordinate teams and individuals not to know the organization's mission and the vision toward the future. Additionally, individuals or teams either may not have well-defined responsibilities or may not understand how their role in the organization supports the overall mission. These types of shortfalls limit an individual's effectiveness to an organization and will be magnified as we discuss principles 2 and 3.

That being said, sometimes all the clarity in the world won't make up for poor processes or inadequate or otherwise inappropriate technology. Another problem I have often seen is when an organization has documented processes with people assigned clear responsibilities and provided the technology to do the job, but still the results fail to meet the mark. Reasons for the limited success or failure vary based on each situation. It may be the result of a shortfall in either number or skill of individuals involved. It may be that the process is unnecessarily cumbersome, so people circumvent the system to save time and energy. Perhaps the technology involved is inappropriate or unreliable. Or possibly, it's a combination of the three. Identifying people, processes, and technology involved in performing a function or task is only the start— what really matters is the end result. If the results are ineffective, then customers will circumvent the system or go elsewhere to get their requirements met. In this context you should consider that everyone has

> **At the end of the day, every function within an organization is founded on people, processes, and technology.**

a customer who they support. If you do not directly interface with your organization's customers then other employees within your organization are your customers. Although external customers are the primary focus of your organization, it is often poor service to internal customers that undermines an organization.

While I was in the Army and assigned to the White House Communications Agency we had formal processes for capturing personnel information using a web-based application. Over time, the process and the application were incorporated into a larger knowledge management (KM) initiative, and we were able to use this personnel information efficiently in other functional areas within the organization. This entire KM effort would eventually be a huge success not just for my direct group, but also for many other organizations with which we collaborated. Much of the success was due to recognizing the value of the personnel information and the importance of being able to use that information in almost every functional aspect of the organization. As we walk through this chapter you will better realize the significance of the information and the commitment to enhance the accuracy and timeliness of making the personnel information available to others within the organization.

Although the end result was great, getting there wasn't exactly easy. The other organizations that were supposed to adopt the system were hesitant to start using it despite our overwhelming success. At the time, our higher headquarters, and other peer level organizations within the command, were not using the web-based capability and were basically using various ad-hoc solutions that they considered best for them to achieve their desired results. They all had problems and inefficiencies centered around inaccurate and untimely information, but each considered those issues far better than the extra work required to "change over" to a new system. They overlooked what may have been small shortfalls for a single internal organization but were enormous knowledge gaps for the enterprise. Further ignored was the fact that implementing the web-based system would actually make their daily lives easier, not more difficult as they assumed, by eliminating duplicated effort, inefficiencies, and inaccuracies.

How does a company solve a problem like this? Consider the root of the problem with respect to an organization's outlook on change as well as lower level leaders who are only concerned with the issues that directly affect their team and no consideration for the larger enterprise effects. Jot down a few ideas of your own related to solving this problem. We'll continue this storyline as we discuss the second and third principles of the LM.

Principle 2: Continual Navigation Involving People, Processes, and Technology Leads to Improvement

It is wise to keep in mind that neither success nor failure is ever final.
- Roger Babson

In the first principle, we talked about how aligning people, processes, and technology with one another and with the organizational mission are critical to company success. So what happens if what worked for a company five years ago doesn't work now? That brings us to our second principle. Successful organizations recognize that they must continually improve if they want to maintain their success. An organization that doesn't make performance improvement a priority will soon find itself irrelevant.

Let's step away from the world of business for a moment and return to the world of sports. I will often use sports comparisons because there are many similarities between sports and business, such as teamwork, competition, and the never-ending quest to get better. Also, I have found many business leaders identify with sports (probably because of the similarities related to teamwork, competition, and continual improvement). Whether you're an individual competitor or a team player, you can't maintain your ranking if you don't continually ramp up your game because new players always come along— often younger players who have the benefit of advances in training techniques— and expectations are forever climbing. Take Tiger Woods for example. Recognized as the number one golfer in the world for many years, Woods continually works on his skills and his process of managing himself and his training on and off the golf course. The technology he uses, not only to play golf but also to improve himself as a golfer and an athlete, is always changing. New clubs and computer-based analytical programs to analyze his swing come to mind. Additionally, he has incorporated various technologies to improve his physical and mental being which will impact his golf game. Tiger Woods is not the same player he was when he first turned pro in 1996— he has advanced with the game.

While I was writing this book, Tiger Woods went through a very tough personal situation made public. I have presented Tiger Woods as an example of an individual who continually seeks performance improvement in his chosen profession and in no other fashion beyond that.

If you want to look at it from a team perspective let's consider the New England Patriots, a team that not only won three Super Bowls in four years between 2001 and 2005, but changed the way many teams approach building a football team in the NFL. During this period, the Patriots maintained a dominant presence, despite losing Pro Bowl-caliber players and coaches. They overcame the loss of key personnel with a strong process for recruiting the right people, training them, and maximizing their strengths while minimizing their weaknesses. They used technology to help them manage these actions, ensuring that every person brought onto their team is the right person for the job and understands his role within the organization. Technology is embedded in all aspects of the game. Software programs are used to evaluate the mental and emotional capacity of players. The use of sophisticated workout equipment to improve the players' physical abilities quickly comes to mind when you think of football. There is the use of advanced video and analytical equipment that enables coaches to monitor their teams, as well as the opponent's tendencies on game day. I want to point out here that in the 2007 NFL season, the Patriots were fined and punished by the NFL for using video equipment to tape defensive signals of their opponents in a manner that was not within the NFL's rules. I am not condoning that any organization should use business practices that are illegal, unethical, or unsafe. I am suggesting that organizations should use recognized, legal practices aggressively to establish and maintain a fair competitive edge.

While discussing the first principle, I mentioned that an individual team member who does not understand his role on the team and how it pertains to the overall mission has a negative impact when it comes to principles 2 and 3. Why is that, you ask? Well, let me ask you a question in return: How can an individual provide valuable input to improving people, processes, or technology if he doesn't understand the ultimate purpose of his role in relation to the mission of the team? You may be able to suggest ways to do your job better, but what is the impact of those changes on the larger organization? Your job may be made easier but you may, in fact, have made other people work harder. Worse yet, without knowing the true value of what you do or the information you provide, you may think it's not important in the big picture and start to focus less energy on something that is actually critical to the organization. Although this is something that will likely be caught down the road, it may not be before significant damage occurs.

In contrast, an individual in touch with his or her role and how it aligns with the organization's mission, regardless of position, can provide valuable insight on how to change people, processes, and/or technology to make true improvements to the organization. The elegance of a holistic approach, such as the LM, is similar to that of a road map; it can point out more than one way to successfully reach your destination— and the LM gives you the means to identify exactly what those alternative routes might be. An approach that addresses the people, processes, and technology of a given situation enables you to consider these three areas to see how you can make improvements to the organization. In one organization, a more aggressive technical approach may be the right way to improve a situation. In another, that solution may not work because of skill shortfalls in the workforce. You may need to take an interim approach of adjusting the process while you address your shortfall with the people in your organization and then come back and reexamine a more technical approach. The bottom line is that the LM provides enormous flexibility to solve problems or to make improvements in performance to maintain your competitive edge.

At the end of our discussion of the first principle, I asked you how you might rectify a situation where personnel information throughout a large enterprise composed of multiple organizations is captured many times over with inaccuracies and inefficiencies. Let's revisit my experience now and see how that plays out. Remember, we had a good web-based solution baseline, but like most technology solutions, it was not ready to solve every unique situation for each sub-organization or individual user out of the box. Additionally, leaders from the personnel and administrative offices did not perceive any major shortfall in their own solutions. The fact that many other people throughout the command were in essence manually collecting the same information on spreadsheets and in databases that already existed in the personnel stove-piped systems was not a shortfall in their mind. After all, this was business as usual. We

> **How can an individual provide valuable input to improving people, processes, or technology if he doesn't understand the ultimate purpose of his role in relation to the mission of the team?**

had various groups of people who were working in silos, unaware of the problems outside of their silo. At the same time, others favored maintaining the status quo despite knowing there were shortfalls that needed to be addressed.

The fact that something "has always been done this way" doesn't mean that the way it's been done is the best way. The first thing we had to do to effect large-scale change was to educate the different organizations in the command on why continual improvement was in their best interest and in the command's best interest. This is the core of the second principle, and central to education is trust and relationship building. Individuals won't benefit from information, however useful it may be, if it comes from a source that lacks authority and validity because they won't feel compelled to apply it. We will delve into building and maintaining strong relationships in detail later in the book.

In my command, we started the educational effort by getting to know the individuals responsible for different aspects of collecting personnel and administrative data. KM analysts that were internal to the organization, as well as external consultants, worked with each user to define each step of their individual processes; specifically, they looked at what information they collected and how, when, and by whom it was used. We found that the personnel and administration section was not the primary source for personnel data, and that when people did use them to acquire information it was only periodically, which meant that updates were not captured consistently. The analysts also worked with end users to identify their pain points, or the parts of their jobs they found difficult or inefficient. By making an effort to understand stakeholders' needs and challenges, analysts developed strong relationships with them and cultivated buy-in for a solution that would address existing individual concerns while improving the entire enterprise.

Continual development and ongoing improvement require relationships and partnerships that empower individuals at all levels to play a part in creating and implementing solutions. Engaging stakeholders means creating a forum to capitalize on individual passions, combine complementary skill sets, and give individuals a feeling of ownership within the organization. These dynamic and cooperative relationships are essential to learning from others' experiences and communicating your own knowledge to others in terms they can understand and appreciate. The outcome? Teams and individuals gain awareness of aspects of the organization and the mission that may never have been on their radar before. They have clarity about how they fit into the larger scheme of things in the business structure. And they understand the value of positive change.

For my command, relationship building and education proved extremely successful. Every organization within the enterprise not only moved to using our personnel and administrative web-based application, but also adopted many other web-based tools that were part of our KM solution. More importantly, they changed because the solution provided operational efficiency and effectiveness that they both benefited from and helped to build— not because they were forced to change.

Principle 3: A Direction Change in People, Processes, or Technology Requires an Azimuth Check of the Other Two

We must become the change we want to see. - Gandhi

If you really think about this third principle, I hope you say to yourself, "How can it be any other way?" If you change a person in the process, at a minimum you will want to at least consider a temporary change to the process itself to provide some additional supervision or coaching until the individual is comfortable in the new role. Likewise, as processes change, maybe because of previously overlooked duplications of effort or new technology, the organization may not need as many people with certain skills but need more people with a different skill set. Finally, consider a situation where a new technology completely eliminates the need for a sub-process altogether, along with the people performing those sub-process tasks. Principle 3 is where organizations truly realize optimal performance and gain efficiencies because it's where they take a big-picture look at their entire operation.

When an organization makes a change in one of our three key areas— people, processes, or technology— without analyzing the impact on the other two areas, efficiencies are only partially realized at best. These types of changes often fail because they are only partial changes; they don't take the entire chain into account, so often there is no gain. Some people may even consider it a waste of time and energy to make the change in the first place. One arena where success can be limited and failure common is the introduction of new technology. Ideally, new technology will be introduced only after relationships are firmly established and stakeholders understand the need for the change. Unfortunately, many organizations focus too much on the technology itself and not enough on the people who will be using it, leading to a poorly executed effort and lots of frustration. Such an incomplete approach leads to limited support at best and counterproductive sabotage of the initiative at worst. As the rate of technology advancement has increased over the years there is more of a mindset that the latest technology is the "silver bullet" that can fix the shortfall at hand. Unrealistic expectations with respect to the time required to make the change lead to shortfalls in training people and accessing processes. This is a leadership issue. If the leader of the organization is fully behind the initiative and can accept the larger investment of time and money that comes with change, the change initiative can be thoroughly executed. If the expectation is that the change will be quick and seamless then often shortcuts will be taken that affect people and processes, appearing as though the change itself was a bad idea.

When an organization repeats a poorly executed change process it can create a poor organizational climate in which employees see these change initiatives as a waste of time. As we will discuss in more detail later in the book, a leader's ability to communicate is so important for an organization and this is especially true when it comes to guiding an organization through change. Because technology drives so many changes for organizations it is easy to see how team members become frustrated when they do not understand the reason the new technology was brought in. An employee's complacency or comfort level may lead him to be unsupportive of the change. Some employees may perceive the technology change as a threat to their jobs and go so far as to sabotage the effort. There have been many a great initiative foiled by poor planning and failure to get people on board with the change.

> **When an organization makes a change in one of our three key areas (people, processes, or technology) without analyzing the impact on the other two areas, efficiencies are only partially realized at best.**

I once did some consulting work for a well-established, small-business government contractor that employed 50 to 75 people. The company provided services in a wide range of general and administrative support and was looking for ways to improve its communications. A common complaint was that there were too many information silos in the company and that many employees were frustrated by the lack of information they had related to the big picture of the company, as well as the different initiatives that were being pursued. It was common for people to be moved from one initiative to another with little forewarning.

The company had a large percentage of people who were comfortable working primarily via email, which exacerbated the communication silos problem. I provided several options to improve the information sharing to include using a commercial-off-the-shelf (COTS) product that would facilitate better information sharing and collaboration on work products. This recommendation, as well as the others, was met with resistance because, ultimately, some of the key people in the organization did not want to do business differently— they just wanted a different result. Eventually, I was able to persuade the leaders that if they did not do business differently, they could not expect a different result. The company moved over to the web application but there was very little effort put toward training people on the application. A small contingent of individuals was slow to adapt to the change and often created large, costly information gaps that affected others who needed their information. The change-over was far more painful than it needed to be. Once again, a poorly planned and executed change initiative made this initiative costly and slow.

How could this situation have been avoided? Attention in two areas would have had a big impact. First, a little more time spent building support within the team through training initiatives and communicating the benefits to them would have helped. Couple that with early adoption by senior leaders and the pace of the change-over increases rapidly. Early adoption by key leaders has a rippling effect throughout an organization.

If we revisit the military organization that I mentioned earlier, we will find that the results were different. In conjunction with the implementation of our web-based personnel and administrative system, and as part of the larger KM effort, people across the entire COI were made part of the solution. Additionally, they not only learned new skills to help them with the technical change but also received clear information about how their efforts and the new system fit into the overall success of the mission. Armed with an understanding of their value in the command and empowered to make changes for the better, organizations streamlined their processes and increased their efficiency dramatically. As part of the overall KM effort, we pushed accurate and timely personnel and administrative information to users who required that information to do their jobs, and they received it when and how they needed it. In the end, the people were happier, the processes were more efficient, and the technology was integrated and fully utilized, making the command increasingly more productive and opening the way for future change.

Conclusion

The three principles discussed in this chapter (and identified in the following summary table) are the foundation of the continual optimization through the LM cycle. Now that we understand the principles and have seen some examples of how they work in action, in the next few chapters we will examine some specific attributes that affect the three principles and an organization's ability to perform its daily business in the most productive manner. Before moving on, the following table captures benefits related to leadership/management, as well as to the organization as a whole, as they relate to the three principles of the LM.

Key concepts and benefits to you as a leader and to the organization

Principle 1 - people, processes, and technology (PP&T) map to every organizational function

Benefits to the Leader/Manager:
- Alignment with strategic goals, mission and vision enables focused leadership
- Facilitates communication of roles and goals to team
- Provides foundation to measure performance of PP&T

Benefits to the Organization:
- Individual roles focused on achieving goals to accomplish mission
- Institutionalizes performance expectations based on roles and goals
- Identifies areas for future organizational improvement

Principle 2 - continual navigation involving people, processes, and technology leads to improvement

Benefits to the Leader/Manager:
- Creates opportunities for improvement – a primary responsibility for leaders
- Empowers leaders to seek alternative ways to improve based on PP&T situation
- Builds on principle 1 enhancing leadership focus

Benefits to the Organization:
- Institutionalizes an organizational culture of continual improvement
- Improvement initiatives are adaptable to each organizational situation – enhancing flexibility
- Enables a synergistic approach to executing an improvement initiative

Principle 3 - a direction change in people, processes, or technology requires an azimuth check of the other two

Benefits to the Leader/Manager:
- Reinforces a holistic approach, accounting for effects to any change initiative

Benefits to the Organization:
- Establishes a thorough improvement process requiring input from all organizational stakeholders

Chapter 3

People - It All Starts With People

Don't tell people how to do things, tell them what to do and let them surprise you with their results.
- George S. Patton

Now that you have had an overview of the LM and the three principles that make up the fundamental nature of the LM, let's look at the key characteristics of people, processes, and technology, which are the foundation of the LM. Starting with people, we will take a look at each key characteristic identified. As I present the key characteristics for people, I want you to remember that each individual is a part of many different organizations when you consider formal organizations and informal COP or COI relationships. Based on this understanding, remember also that each individual has responsibilities that are aligned with leadership skills and management skills. Finally, remember that regardless of your role in an organization or COI you have some type of planning and execution responsibility in performing a mission. Simply put, the LM recognizes that each individual on the team has similar responsibilities with respect to being a leader, manager, and team member, depending on each unique situation.

When all is said and done it starts with people. Great people executing an average plan are more likely to get great results as opposed to average people executing a great plan. The following characteristics discussed are what I consider to be the most important characteristics for people, either individually or within a team setting. These characteristics

have close ties to other qualities that make people happy and productive in an organizational setting.

Trustworthiness

Few things help an individual more than to place responsibility upon them and to let them know that you trust them. - Booker T. Washington

I cannot think of anything more important in a relationship than trust. Stephen Covey's books have captured this truth in several fashions.

It is reasonable to say that if you have read any professional development material covering leadership, management, or personal development, it is likely that trust is identified as an essential element for success. The reason for this is simple— if you do not have a relationship based on trust you do not have a relationship that can reach its full potential. I have enjoyed many aspects of Stephen Covey's work and particularly his material regarding relationships and trustworthiness. His message is clear, concise, and serves as a fundamental element of building a strong relationship. The following is his story from my perspective.

In Stephen Covey's book, *The 7 Habits of Highly Effective People*, he discusses how essential trust is to any relationship. Covey talks about trust using a bank account analogy. He calls it an emotional bank account. Think in terms of how your actions are either deposits or withdrawals into the account that affects how your trustworthiness is judged within a relationship. Positive actions are deposits and negative actions are withdrawals to the relationship. I do not intend to repeat all the points Covey makes in regard to how essential trust is within an organization, but I will briefly walk through the six methods that Covey identifies as ways to make deposits into the emotional bank account.

1. Seek to understand the other person from their point of view. Covey talks about how the sincere effort to get to know an individual and what is important to that individual establishes a foundation of trust. The effort to get to know someone is no small task and demonstrates how important that individual is to you. What makes this challenging is that we tend to view matters from our life's experiences and may not fully appreciate that someone else's experiences may be why they have a different view on a particular issue.

2. Attending to the little things has a big impact on the emotional bank account. Covey emphasizes that small acts of kindness go a long way to strengthening your relationship but unkind actions tend to make an even larger withdraw from the emotional bank account.

3. Keeping commitments or promises. A promise is considered to be almost a contract. When you break a promise it is a major withdraw from the emotional account. As you can imagine, this is particularly true with children.

4. Clarifying expectations limits the possibility for withdrawals from the emotional bank account. Covey's point being that often people do not understand their roles or responsibilities in a relationship. Defining the expectation ensures the two parties know what is expected of each other, building trust faster.

5. Showing personal integrity. Leading in a manner in which your words are aligned with your actions demonstrates high personal integrity. One of Covey's points is that you should treat or talk about people the same whether they are present or not.

6. Sincere apology. When we fall short of expectations and make a withdraw from the account, a sincere apology can help to repair the damage. However, if these shortfalls become a habit, then the apologies become meaningless and are actually withdraws.

The above points are hard to argue against. The LM in its simplest form recognizes interactions with people as a critical component to success and embraces trust as the most important criteria. With the above in mind, I want to highlight that trust is a two-way street. Too often people see trust as being a one-way street. It is likely that if you do not trust someone you have a professional or personal relationship with they probably feel the same toward you. So, first and foremost, look to see what you can do to fix the situation. The effects of an atmosphere of low trust within an organization are very damaging. Trust directly affects communication. Information often is not shared as openly as it should be when there is little or no trust. People tend to hold their cards close to their vest for fear that the information will be used in some manner that will either negatively impact them or positively affect the individuals whom they do not trust and probably do not like. It is easy to see how quickly the organization can become fractured, ultimately leading to negative operational performance without trust as the foundation.

A solid relationship based on trust enables individuals to open up and share information without worrying about being ridiculed or receiving other unfavorable actions. This foundation of trust creates an environment for optimal performance and, most important, for ideas to flow continually, stimulates innovation and optimization. Without a foundation of trust many good ideas remain unspoken, where they are safe from ridicule or risk of failure.

Based on my experience, as well as many others, trust is the most important characteristic regarding people. The difficulty is that trust is built over time and, if you are new to an organization or affiliation with a group of people, you can expect to be tested either consciously or subconsciously by individuals with regard to trustworthiness. Further, remember that your trustworthiness will be tested every day in every encounter that you have. If you think you will pass every time you are wrong. Nobody goes through life without saying or doing something they will later regret. Remember that you are human and sometimes emotion gets the best of you. Too often we react emotionally and impulsively in a manner that is inappropriate or deceitful. We have all done this but what we don't all do is go back and try to rectify the situation with a response that explains why we reacted how we did and that, in hindsight, we were wrong.

A **reaction** is more impulsive in nature and, depending on the circumstances, may not at all reflect how you really feel. We have all been in an emotional debate with someone or a group of people and blurted out something that really does not reflect how we feel but provides some type of immediate sense of satisfaction or vindication of some sort. A **response**, on the other hand, is something that is more carefully thought out and hopefully better reflects how we really feel. Having said that, responses too can be inappropriate and deceitful, which in turn is far more damaging when it comes to relationships.

I encourage you to look at how you conduct yourself and continually look at ways to become a model when it comes to trustworthiness. Because we are human we will all make mistakes; it is our response to these mistakes that makes the difference when it comes to building a relationship based on trust. Remember Covey's point of sincere apology. Consider how you as a leader are viewed when you make an error. How might your mistake taint someone's view of you? A good litmus test is to honestly assess your conduct with an independent third party perspective. If you cannot be honest with yourself then imagine how hard it is to have an open and honest relationship with others.

What can an organization do to help create a trustworthy

> **A solid relationship based on trust allows individuals to open up and share information without worrying about being ridiculed or receiving other unfavorable actions.**

environment? It starts with leaders who serve as strong role models. Formal leaders must serve as models in how they live their lives and conduct themselves. However, even if you work for a leader that may not display trustworthy actions, do not let that affect how you conduct yourself. Remember that leadership based on the whole person is far more influential then leadership based on position. Your trustworthiness and other strong character traits strengthen your role as a leader.

Considering Covey's points discussed earlier, here are four habits that help promote an environment of trust within an organization.

1. Lead by example: You must live a life of integrity, setting an example by your actions. You control your actions and this is how you are judged by others with whom you interact. Every interaction you have is in essence a test of your character.

2. Treat people how you want to be treated (the Golden Rule): Treat people in a respectful manner and in a way that you would like to be treated if you were in their situation. Covey's point of being able to understand a person from their perspective will help you as a leader to take this gesture to the next level. One practice to help promote an environment where people treat each other in a respectful and fair manner is to write off honest mistakes without ridicule and without harboring long lasting feelings. An honest mistake can be rectified and lessons can be learned. If handled correctly, an honest mistake can strengthen the trust in a relationship and the organization as a whole.

3. Confront trust issues swiftly: In order to be effective when dealing

with trust issues you must be someone who can be trusted. Building from the first two points, when there is an issue, it is important to address it head on and either clear the air or take appropriate actions so that it will not damage the rest of the organization. Remember that if you are a true leader, it is your responsibility to confront the other person when an issue involving trust arises.

Issues of trust are best resolved when dealt with in an open and matter of fact manner. The following story provides an example of how to deal with an issue in which your trust of an individual may have been damaged. Put yourself in Jan's shoes and consider how you would handle this situation. Jan, a 37 year-old regional sales manager for a national manufacturing company, notices that Steve, a 32 year-old sales representative working for her, has started to show a pattern of missing meetings. The problem was exacerbated when he missed a meeting during which he was supposed to provide a presentation to other sales representatives related to a new product line coming out in a few weeks. Steve is Jan's leading sales representative, which is why she chose him to lead this effort in the first place. Despite his recent failure to make scheduled meetings, Steve's sales performance is still the best among the representatives. Is missing meetings a concern? His performance is still the best; do you ignore this longer? If it were not Steve would you have already acted? These are the types of questions that a leader is faced with continually.

Action is always better than inaction. Action in any situation, as is the case in this example, can and should start with collecting more information to understand the circumstances. Jan must confront Steve and ask him questions so that she has the information needed to decide whether anything needs to be done at this point. Looking at the LM map, we are talking about the arrow between the Leader and the team that represents communication. Based on the communication between Jan and Steve, Jan learns that Steve sees these meetings as a waste of time and he points out that his sales numbers are the best on the team, so he has demonstrated his competence and should not need to attend the meeting. Although Jan does not like the answer, she puts herself in Steve's position and can understand why he may view these meetings as unproductive from his perspective.

Armed with information and understanding the situation from Steve's perspective, Jan can take appropriate action. She recognizes that Steve's perspective is limited in scope and the issue is not one of trust, related to his doing what he thinks is right for productivity, but that he needs to better understand the issue from a broader perspective. Jan discusses the importance of the meeting to the others who are not performing as well as Steve and that these meetings are designed to advance the team as a whole. She further communicates that she chose Steve to lead the new product line presentation because of his superb performance in the past. Jan then more effectively communicated to Steve that she wants him to not only lead the introduction of the new product line but wants to empower him to help the other sales representatives improve their performance. Step two of the LM is now in motion. Steve is going to develop and execute a plan to make the other sales representatives more productive. As Steve starts to execute the plan, Jan uses her management skills to monitor and measure the results of Steve's programs (the third step of the LM).

As you would suspect, after step three of the LM, Jan starts the three-step cycle again, providing feedback to Steve so that he and the sales representatives can adjust the program to further enhance sales performance. In this example, a concern that had started to affect Jan's trust of Steve not only was resolved but was turned into a positive for the organization.

4. Avoid organizational trustworthiness issues with good hiring practices: The final point I want to stress is that thoughtful, proactive hiring is the best approach to avoiding trust issues. If you have control over the people that you bring into your organization, then you have an opportunity to positively influence the trustworthy factor of the organization. First, do not compromise on issues of character when it comes to hiring people. If they have problems from the past, get an explanation and try to get other perspectives of the problem. A problem in the past is different from a pattern of questionable behavior.

I consider character traits to be far more important than skill and knowledge, when it comes to putting someone on my team. Where possible, bring in people with whom you already have an established relationship. It amazes me how quick people are to cast off individuals whom they know, because of minor issues with skill or knowledge, in favor of someone they do not know because his resume is more impressive. I would rather know a person and his limitations than to have to learn a new person's limitation. When you need to bring in a new team member, see if there are options available that will make it possible for you to establish a relationship before you bring them on full time. This is not only beneficial to you but to the new person who may find out that this job is not a good fit.

Trust is critical in all relationships and with a strong organizational climate that has a foundation of trust, individuals and the team as a whole will flourish. The time and energy spent to hire, train, and retain trustworthy people will pay off many times over for the organizations that you can influence.

To close each discussion related to the characteristics of people, processes, and technology, I will provide sample questions that can be used to conduct what I call an "azimuth check assessment." The intent is to use these questions to perform assessments on a recurring basis. These assessments are just another tool that is in keeping with the spirit of the LM's cyclic approach for continual improvement.

The following questions, combined with a formal personnel performance evaluation system, can help you understand your organizational cli-

People – Azimuth Check
Trust
What activities occur that provide opportunities to build relationships and trust? Are these recurring events? Are there individuals who routinely do not participate? Why?
Assess the overall environment related to trust by asking team members these questions:
Do you feel the leaders of the organization are trustworthy?
Do you think that the team environment promotes openness and honesty?
Do you sense that issues of trust have been dealt with appropriately?
What character considerations are made during the hiring process?
Are roles and goals used within the organization to help define expectations?
Are character training opportunities provided that can help establish and maintain trust within the organization? What additional activities can be included and why?

mate and implement initiatives to help establish and maintain an organizational climate built on trust.

Passion

We may affirm absolutely that nothing great in the world has been accomplished without passion. - Hegel

Passion is a quality that can make an average performer great. Whenever a person is able to work in an area they are passionate about they are bound to give you everything they have to offer. Soon we will talk about knowledge and skill, which are both required for an individual to be successful. However, without passion it is not likely that knowledgeable and skilled people will meet their full potential. As you look at what you are doing for your organization, and what members of your team are doing, keep in mind that people tend to work best in areas that they are passionate about. When you are considering hiring a new employee or putting a person in a new position, you should make passion a primary consideration above knowledge and skill.

A passionate individual tends to spend an enormous amount of time and energy learning about the particular subject area and refining their skills. So although they may not be the most knowledgeable or skilled individual in the equation today, their passion to become better will quickly change that situation. A passionate person will take advantage of a training/development program or other opportunities to improve individual knowledge and skill. Less passionate individuals are not likely to make the effort to continually improve upon their knowledge and skill levels. As time goes on, the less passionate individual's knowledge and skill become dated and maybe even obsolete.

What are the long term effects of having passionate individuals on your team? My experience is that the effects are primarily positive for the organization. Passionate individuals tend to become better at their profession. This desire leads to innovation and change, which keeps the organization looking at better ways to do business and leads to more efficient and effective business practices. If this type of person also has strong leadership skills the organizational atmosphere is greatly enhanced. A passionate leader at any level can have an impact up, across, and down organizational hierarchies. This impact can affect business practices in all areas to include training and development programs for others. This impact multiplies the positive effects many times over. A passionate person operates very comfortably in an organization that is driven by the empowering principles of the LM, which promote continual improvement.

Like many things in life, there can be too much of a good thing. When passion becomes extremism then not only are the positive effects associated with passion lost, normally negative impacts can be expected in some fashion. An extreme focus in a particular area limits the ability to see issues from other perspectives. This limited perspective does not allow you as a leader to understand how other team members view issues and, before you know it, you are not receiving any feedback from individuals who do not share your view.

An extremist leader quickly develops a myopic view of their profession and does not possess the ability to see the damaging effects on the organization. Maybe you have a personal experience where you observed a leader whose overzealous approach was more damaging than it

> **Passionate individuals tend to become better at their profession. This desire leads to innovation and change, which keeps the organization looking at better ways to do business...**

was constructive? I have experienced this as well. On a few occasions I have seen overbearing leaders who almost crippled their organizations through an overzealous approach that stifled initiative and even left competent individuals questioning their ability. There is no reason to go into great detail discussing the damage these individuals did to the morale, productivity, and growth of the organization. Just keep in mind that even Jack Welch (former CEO of General Electric and noted expert on leadership), a self-proclaimed workaholic, recognizes that there needs to be some type of work-life balance to keep a balanced perspective. "If there was ever a case of 'Do as I say, not as I did,' this is it. No one, myself included, would ever call me an authority on work-life balance. For 41 years, my operating principle was work hard, play hard, and spend some time as a father." Sure, being overzealous in a particular area can have a negative impact in other areas of your life if you allow it. However, the positives of passion far outweigh the negative aspect as long as you maintain a balanced foundation on life and fall back on principles to help guide you in your daily interactions. Passion brings natural energy that just needs to be harnessed appropriately.

I can think of many personal experiences with respect to passion. In the Introduction I spoke of my passion for the subject of leadership. This book represents a work of passion. My zeal for the subject explains the time I invested in learning and teaching different aspects of leadership in formal and informal settings. My enthusiasm for leadership enables me to continually seek opportunities to learn more and to look for opportunities to lead people. If you become more passionate about all the components of being a leader it will enhance your effectiveness and increase your ability to achieve success.

As a consultant, I am exposed to many organizations and leaders. Although in these circumstances I am brought into the organization to provide my expertise, I always leave the job having learned something from the others involved. I have picked up many great template check lists to facilitate a particular work product. I have even picked up simple techniques in how to more efficiently run a meeting or how to get introverted people involved in a brainstorming session. If you desire to become a better leader, you must learn from every opportunity that presents itself. This realization is not unique to leadership but applies to any subject for which you are passionate. The opportunities to learn time-saving management techniques and effective ways to build relationships present themselves daily— are you paying attention?

I was fortunate enough to work with a group of extremely talented scientists. I was helping them with a strategy to win grant money to expand their ability to conduct rare isotope research. I know nothing about the subject but was there to help them capture their ideas in a manner that could communicate to a board that it was in the U.S. Government's best interest to fund the expansion of their rare isotope research facility. Several of the scientists I worked with were internationally recognized in their particular field. As I worked with these individuals, I could see the true passion they had for the science and for the project. Several of the scientists had spent almost 10 years looking at the best way to expand the ability to research rare isotopes. It was this true passion our team captured that would ultimately provide the compelling argument to the board.

One of the ways we capitalized on this passion was to have them intimately involved in writing the proposal. You may think that this is a given, but I have worked on other proposals where the people involved were not passionate about the subject and it was difficult to get quality information from them. In those situations it is almost easier to leave them out of much of the process and only seek their expertise for factual information. However, in this case, involving the scientists in the proposal writing process not only improved the team's understanding of the subject but, more important, the scientists' zeal was infectious to the proposal team and helped us create a far better proposal. For example, I would often ask the scientists to just tell me about a particular issue or challenge that they would routinely face and how they would overcome that challenge. I would ask follow-up questions related to their solution and invite them to explain the benefits of their solution. Within this discussion valuable nuggets of information would surface that I could then ask them to further expand. The combination of their expertise and passion (these two characteristics go hand-in-hand) enabled them to provide a unique and very valuable perspective.

From an organizational perspective, you want to harness the power that comes with passion. It starts with getting the right people and putting them in the right positions within the organization. This will be discussed in more detail when we talk about complementary placement of people in an organization. Additionally, if the organization has successfully created an environment of trust, people are more likely to jump into their jobs without fear of making mistakes; this, in turn, stimulates individuals to take ownership of responsibilities and creates a passion to succeed. Similar to hiring people that are trustworthy, your ability to hire people who exude a passionate but also a balanced approach to life is always a great start.

Passion can further be created by empowering people to execute initiatives that are in line with the second and third principles of the LM. We will talk in more detail about empowerment later. The point is that when you create ownership and empower individuals at all levels to go beyond just doing their jobs and encourage them to find ways to improve their results this is a powerful win-win scenario. It is this type of passion that feeds the next key characteristic that we will discuss, which is knowledge and skill. As part of your azimuth check assessment, use the following questions to help you monitor your own and the organizational environment with respect to the characteristic of passion.

People – Azimuth Check

Passion

	Assess how passionate the individuals on your team are about their role.
·	
	Did each individual have input on their roles and the goals?
	Do the goals reflect a passion for their role? Would you consider some of the goals to reflect a desire for self improvement?
	Do you sense an overall upbeat organizational climate that is normally present with a healthy passion for the organization's mission?
	Do you and members of your team also have alternative interests outside of your primary role in this organization? Are there activities designed to promote pursuit of those interests or alternative views and ideas within your primary role with the company? Do these alternatives help to prevent myopic views that can develop from overzealous focus on any one subject?

Knowledge & Skill

It is possible to fly without motors, but not without knowledge and skill.
- Wilbur Wright

Knowledge and skill normally have a strong association but they are not the same. **Knowledge** is an understanding of a subject based on experience and/or education. **Skill** is the ability to perform a task or a series of tasks at some level of competence. You may have knowledge of a subject but lack the skill to perform the tasks required to produce the desired results in that specific area. Leaders/managers often know about a subject from a broader perspective but frequently do not have the skills to perform each individual task required for success. The best analogy to demonstrate this would be a coach in relationship to a player in any sport. Consider a football coach, who may or may not have played football but still has knowledge regarding football strategy and specific position training techniques. Bill Belichick comes to mind as a very successful coach who never played football professionally. It is important to point out that coaching itself (like leadership and management) does require skill. For example, communication skills are essential for leading an organization or coaching a team. The point is that knowledge and skill are closely related and, regardless of what your role is within an organization, it requires knowledge and skill of some sort. The most successful leaders/ managers/team members are constantly looking at how to improve both knowledge and skill.

My experience is that knowledge and skill are closely associated with competence. Where trust and passion may make you a likeable person whom everyone is rooting for to succeed, competence is the key ingredient to achieving the desired results. With the exception of luck, it is impossible to succeed as an individual or a team without knowledge of what needs to be done and the skill set to get those things done. The good news is that knowledge and specific skills are much easier to acquire for passionate people, which is why I stated earlier that I would favor hiring a less experienced individual who demonstrates a passion to succeed than a more experienced individual who has not demonstrated a passion to sharpen his skills or continue to study his profession.

Becoming proficient within any profession requires continual education. For example, as we discussed earlier, to become a good leader you must continually seek improvement and development as a professional. Many public and private sector organizations have formalized professional development programs that balance institutional education with operational experience. This approach provides an individual with the best opportunity for a successful career by continually broadening knowledge and learning theory within an institutional setting and then using operational assignments to enhance skills that were introduced in those settings. Furthermore, this approach provides the organization with the best

> **The most successful leaders/managers/team members are constantly looking at how to improve both knowledge and skill.**

opportunity for success. An organization that provides a methodical professional development approach for its employees is one that will attract that passionate person we mentioned previously, who will want to take advantage of the opportunity for self improvement. This, in turn, is good for the organization, which benefits from a more knowledgeable and better skilled employee.

For example, during my Army career, I was provided with more than four years of institutional educational opportunities spread between operational assignments. These educational opportunities enhanced my performance during operational assignments and also created a mindset of learning as a life-long endeavor.

How does an organization help itself to create knowledgeable and skilled personnel? First, find people who possess character traits that demonstrate their willingness to continually get better at what they do. If that individual already comes with a high level of competency, that is a plus, but if not, you can easily fix that situation. You can enhance competency by creating an organizational climate that provides opportunities for individuals to seek self improvement. This can be accomplished by offsetting educational costs as well as establishing an organizational professional development program. Second, recognize and reward individuals who seek self improvement informally and formally. Recognition of an educational milestone can range from informal acknowledgement to financial bonuses. I also encourage making self-improvement an important criterion when it comes to promotion.

Some may say if I hired the passionate person you suggested, I do not need to provide this type of incentive program based on the individual's drive to improve. This is probably true, but we all like to be rewarded for our accomplishments. The reality of the situation is that every organization wants those passionate people and many of those organizations are willing to help them become better at their profession. To be competitive for such talent you need to offer some educational incentives. Also consider the message you are sending in the bigger picture. You reward results and behavior that support your core beliefs and mission so why would you not reward someone who is trying to become better in his profession and enhance their performance for your team? I do not know who said this but I once saw a tag line at the bottom of a co-worker's email that said, "If you think training is expensive, imagine what the cost is to have untrained people."

One of my observations in working with small businesses is that they struggle to attract and retain high caliber people who want to further their education and professional development. Small businesses often cannot offer the same type of educational benefits that a larger company does. I encourage the small businesses to try and use other types of incentives to attract the people or, even better, to work with a human resource firm to help create better opportunities for employee educational benefits. When you have employees that are taking advantage of educational benefits you have the right type of employees. As part of your azimuth check assessment, use the following questions to help you monitor your own and the

People – Azimuth Check

Knowledge and Skill

Does the organization offer attractive incentives for individuals to seek improvements in knowledge and skill?	
Are there organizational and individual goals associated with continual education?	
Are there organizational and individual incentives and goals related to skill proficiency? Can these incentives tie directly to organizational efficiency and/or effectiveness?	
Does the organization have any type of sponsorship or mentorship program so that less-experienced employees can gain knowledge from more-experienced employees?	
Is there a knowledge-sharing program that allows "best practices" to be shared within the organization? What can be done to improve the sharing of knowledge?	

organizational environment with respect to the characteristic of knowledge and skill.

Complementary

Talent wins games, but teamwork and intelligence win championships.
- Michael Jordan

Up to this point we have talked about key characteristics of individuals and how individuals with these key characteristics can provide great service to the organization. The complementary characteristic applies to the organization or team. No matter how much individual talent you have on a team, the members still need to perform together in a complementary manner to achieve sustained success. A baseball team comprised of the most talented infielders available is not likely to fare as well as a team with average talent but skills that are appropriate for every position on the field. We can take this analogy one step further. I will suggest that a team with less talented individuals positioned in a complementary manner will outperform a team with more talent that has been positioned with no regard to how their talents complement each other. A business similarly requires people with various skill sets and knowledge to succeed. The key to this success is getting the right combination of those people working together.

I admire Jim Collins' work and how he presents information related to building a successful team. His work spanned years of research and has been considered one of the best studies related to building a successful organization. If you have read Jim Collins book, *Good to Great*, then this should not be a surprise to you. In his book, Collins first talks about the importance of putting "who" before "what," or in other words, getting good people on your team is more important than determining what you are going to do with those people. He later states that once you have the right people on the "bus" you need to ensure that they are in the right "seat." Collins' point is that it is more than just placing people in a position based on skill and knowledge qualifications; they must be the right person (who). A person who demonstrates character and passion with a willingness to help the organization succeed can do much for an organization in almost any position. Once you have that type of person, you can really get the most he or she has to offer by putting them in a position that will magnify their talents and team them with others who will not just offset their weaknesses, but who will help strengthen these weaknesses. Based on my experience in leading organizations and coaching youth sports I could not agree more with Collins' proclamation.

The concept of building a team with complementary skills seems so basic yet it is often overlooked. Going back to what we previously discussed with regard to trust, passion, knowledge, and skill it should be easier to see why you want to select a less talented person who has high trust and passion over an individual with more talent but who lacks passion. One such example would be if you were filling a position within a team that already had a high level of competency. Depending on the people involved, this teaming arrangement may be the most productive because it gives others an opportunity to lead and teach this individual, which is a win-win situation for all involved. A leader needs to understand this and be able to look at the people dynamics that are involved when it comes to the creation and employment of teams. Certain people perform well in certain situations or when teamed with certain types of people. For you, as a leader, to get the most from your team, you must understand the people dynamics of the equation. It starts with what we talked about earlier concerning trust. Your understanding of what makes a person tick will enable you to put that individual and the team in the best position to succeed. If you are in an organization that often assembles teams of people for specific tasks (a COP or COI approach) this is a key component of success.

Another more challenging aspect of building a complementary team is being able to work with people who have differences of opinion or different perspectives. Often these differences stand in the way of coming to agreement and some leaders see these differences as problems. The most talented leaders will see these differences as an opportunity to create a better solution that considers the different perspectives. The challenge lies in the leader's ability to accept the differences in opinion and to communicate within the team that these differences are not only OK but can provide an added bonus to the solution.

A leader's/ manager's ability to po-

> **The concept of building a team with complementary skills seems so basic yet it is often overlooked.**

sition talent in a complementary manner is a strong asset and works in concert with the continual adjustment approach among people, processes, and technology that makes up the second and third principles of the LM. The nature of the LM requires an attentiveness to how people's skills and attitudes complement each other within the designated processes and the technology available in performing individual and team tasks that support the overall mission.

My first experience with an organization that really tried to take the time to hire and assign individuals in a holistic manner was as a major in the Army when I served with a very elite special operations organization. Because this unit was such a high priority organization within the big picture of national security, we were able to get the best people available. We had a very demanding selection process that included several interviews with peer groups, lower level section leaders, and upper level leadership. This was standard protocol for all individuals who wanted an assignment to the unit. Across the board, regardless of position, there seemed to be a tendency to get high caliber people who were self starters and possessed qualities normally associated with leadership. This tendency generally served the organization well; however, on a few occasions we hired too many people who were too alike and lost the complementary perspective that would enhance the team and allow us to see issues from other perspectives.

Within my consulting business, I often see organizational leaders who do not fully appreciate the benefit of having other perspectives, ideas, or approaches to solving a particular problem. Too often these leaders are stuck on "how" to accomplish the objective and find it difficult to appreciate alternative methods. This lack of appreciation sometimes goes so far as the leader habitually dismissing people with alternative views and often surrounding themselves with individuals who almost always tend to agree with them (commonly referred to as "yes men"). The lack of alternative perspectives limits the organization's ability to adjust or perform at a higher level, whereas the ability to capitalize on people who have different views and bring them into the situation in a complementary manner will create a better solution in the bigger picture.

How can an organization ensure that they have complementary talents working together to create a win-win situation? The LM is designed exactly for this purpose. Regardless of the situation the people part of the equation needs to be considered. Putting the right person in a position is very dependent on the personalities, character traits, and skill set of everyone within the team. As you look at the LM diagram from Chapter 1 (*Figure 1*), consider the continual analytical nature of the LM with respect to the leader/manager communicating expectations as well as monitoring and measuring performance. As you work within this framework a primary consideration should be obtaining the complementary balance of people who possess the right skills, knowledge, and attitude to perform within the processes and with the technology available. Much of this is process oriented and will be further discussed in Chapter 4 when we talk about processes. Note that a key process that is often overlooked for setting expectations and providing feedback involves the use of personnel performance evaluations and recurring meetings focused on individual and team performance. If the manager part of your brain has collected information and measured performance, the leader within you needs to close that loop with performance feedback that can be used to further enhance the performance of individuals and teams. This feedback should be constructive in nature, whether it is positive or negative. Expectations should have already been communicated formally and informally. How did the team and the individuals perform? If there are shortfalls you must ask why and how can we fix the shortfalls. The answer lies within the framework of the LM and making adjustments related to the dynamics of people, processes, and technology. Making adjustments to one of those three areas (principle 2) will fix the shortfall.

Use the LM and the recurring azimuth check assessment to help guide your ability and others within your organization to take advantage of creating and maintaining a complementary team that can create powerful solutions. The following can help keep the characteristic of a complementary team at the forefront of your overall personnel management practices and leadership style.

People – Azimuth Check

Complementary

	Have the required skills and knowledge been identified and broken down into tasks that support our mission? Have these been captured in our position descriptions?
	Do the people we have filling the positions possess the skills and knowledge required?
	Do we do a good job of using our personnel performance evaluations and recurring counseling sessions to maintain a focus of the three individual characteristics: trust, passion, and skill/knowledge?
	Do you see opportunities to assemble action teams to solve problems that take advantage of the three individual characteristics (trust, passion, and skill/knowledge)?
	Does the leadership take advantage of the talents of the individual to create complementary teams? How?
	How receptive is leadership to difference of opinion on how to solve problems?
	Are there mechanisms and recurring forums in place to allow for team communications that facilitate brainstorming, and consensus on solution for execution?

Empowerment

I start with the premise that the function of leadership is to produce more leaders, not more followers. - Ralph Nader

The final people characteristic that I will discuss is empowerment. An organization is only able to realize its full potential if it can successfully empower the team members to do the things that they need to do to succeed. This type of approach to performing an organization's mission starts with a climate of trust and it builds upon the foundation created from the other people characteristics we already discussed. Just as trust starts with senior leaders so does empowerment. Empowerment is a natural transformation for passionate people to accept. Assuming that you have formed a complementary team with the right knowledge and skill, empowering that team to perform is the final step that enables them not to just do their job but to continually look at ways to do it better. I am sure most seasoned leaders recognize the strong arguments of what is stated here. The question is do these leaders' actions reflect the rhetoric they may preach when it comes to empowerment?

It is a special leader who can honestly create the type of environment that pushes people to become their best and is able to write off honest mistakes that come from a high energy team that is looking to continually get better. 3M is such a company and has used this approach almost since its inception in 1902. The Minnesota Mining and Manufacturing Co. (3M) was founded to mine a mineral deposit for grinding-wheel abrasives. After struggling for years the company mastered quality production and a supply chain, attracting new investors that led to early technical and marketing innovations and long-term success. 3M's climate of innovation and change has been the subject of many studies and articles.

3M's success revolves around principles that were created in 1948 and are closely aligned with many of the ideas presented in this book. They empower people and teams and encourage creativity through different formal and informal programs. Over the years the names of the programs may change but ultimately the intent remains the same:

- Encourage employees to show initiative and determine their path to success
- Empower teams to be able to operate autonomously
- Promote and encourage informal collaborations
- Institutionalize innovation by sharing with others

William L. McKinight's basic rule of management was captured in 1948 and remains a cornerstone of 3M management philosophy today:

"As our business grows, it becomes increasingly necessary to delegate responsibility and to encourage men and women to exercise their initiative. This requires considerable tolerance. Those men and women to whom we delegate authority and responsibility, if they are good people, are going to want to do their jobs in their own way.

"Mistakes will be made. But if a person is essentially right, the mistakes he or she makes are not as serious in the long run as the mistakes management will make if it undertakes to tell those in authority exactly how they must do their jobs.

"Management that is destructively critical when mistakes are made kills initiative. And it's essential that we have many people with initiative if we are to continue to grow."

I have been fortunate enough to work for several leaders who understood the importance of empowerment. I like to think that I am that type of leader; the true judges of that are the people you lead. Leaders can get results without this type of approach but what are the long term disadvantages of not taking an approach that allows for future leaders to be developed?

I think it is obvious that an approach that does not empower junior people will eventually limit the organization's growth. Specifically, the team becomes more dependent on one or two leaders who need to see everything before action is taken. I have seen organizations come almost to a standstill because even minor decisions in the big picture are elevated to a senior level for resolution. In addition to the effects on

> **It is a special leader who can honestly create the type of environment that pushes people to become their best and is able to write off honest mistakes...**

timely production, this type of atmosphere communicates a lack of trust, as well as ignores opportunities to develop junior leaders. The stagnation in operational issues and leader development really starts to show itself in situations when the key leaders are not available, and more importantly years later when the organization's personnel pipeline is empty when it comes to qualified leaders who know the specifics of the organization. Like many reading this book, I have seen many examples of empowering leaders, as well as the other extreme with leaders who may talk the talk but whose actions do not reflect their words.

My experience is that more people talk the talk than walk the walk when it comes to empowerment. I once witnessed two senior individuals within a small company debate the placement of a table on a diagram that was being used to represent a floor layout for an upcoming event. The junior person went well above and beyond his duty to put together a very comprehensive plan for our organization's participation in an upcoming event and now the senior leader was questioning the depiction of where the table would be located. A 30-minute argument over the planned placement of the table in a 10x10 cubicle ended with both individuals angry about the other's perspective of the table placement. Again, this was over a diagram where the table might be placed in an event a month away.

I later confronted the more senior of the two and asked why he was so concerned about this diagram. He went back to his argument about the best use of space and other points which he had made earlier. I replied that I was not talking about the merits of the argument; I was talking about why he would argue about this at all. I asked if he trusted the person putting together the event to be able to do this. He immediately said he did. Did he think that he is talented enough to figure out the best place put a table for such an event? He said not based on the diagram. I further suggested that if the table was put in the wrong place, I was confident that the individual would recognize this in a short amount of time and be able to very easily rectify the situation on site in less than 30 seconds. I also shared with the more senior leader that if he really had issue with the placement of the table, instead of telling the other person where to place the table he could have first tried to get a better understanding of why he placed the table there. That type of an approach at least gives you the benefit of understanding the thought process behind this decision. During the course of the conversation, I explained that it had been my experience that even if you may not agree with minor aspects of a plan (such as the placement of a table), it is often better to let it run its course and let individuals learn first-hand from a plan they put together and executed. You tend to learn more from an experience when you have "skin in the game." If it is your plan you are accountable for the results versus if you are executing a plan that you didn't help develop, or worse yet, don't buy into. Although he agreed, I was never sure if he really understood that more is learned from first-hand mistakes than from second-hand success.

As I mentioned, I have often seen more leaders hesitant to empower their people than leaders who will. The reason is normally because senior leaders feel responsible for what happens and often cannot watch someone do something differently than they would have done it. Moreover, they believe failure reflects poorly on them and they are not willing to walk around in the short term with a "black eye" if they did not give it to themselves.

An organization that is more closely aligned with the 3M model mentioned earlier is where you will witness true innovation. The empowerment of team members creates an environment in which good ideas can grow. My past had exposed me to situations in which, when problems occurred within a change initiative, weak leaders or short-term thinkers were quick to pull the plug or take a step backwards as opposed to a bold step forward. I was pleasantly surprised during my time at the White House Communications Agency when the commander I worked for was different— he was truly an empowering leader and encouraged people to take action in difficult situations. Of the many great things this commander did, the one that sticks out the most to me was when we "officially" rolled out our new KM initiative that I spoke of earlier in the book. After substantial work on a beta test we boldly went live across the enterprise. There was no doubt that the coordination for the roll out was weak at best and I even believe that it somewhat caught the commander off guard. The poor coordination effort created an even larger than normal contingent of grumblers who did not like the new initiative. Some of those grumbling were senior level leaders within organizations that we supported. Our commander took the brunt of the blow and did not turn around and pass it down to the subordinate leaders or the individuals who had been working this aggressive initiative. The commander walked around proudly with his black eye because he knew in the long term this was the right move, despite the poor coordination effort and other shortfalls that were minor in nature when compared to the entire KM effort.

The commander was right and within a year WHCA and the supported organizations had completely changed the way they did business. Efficiencies and effectiveness of all the organizations steadily improved over the course of a few years. Three years after the initial launch day, the KM initiative was awarded a Defense Information Systems Agency award for innovation and effectiveness. Many great people were empowered to make this endeavor the success it was. With that said, the steadfast leadership of the commander was the key to this success. I have seen too many other leaders who would not have been able to let this run its course based on the shaky start.

Creating an organizational environment that takes advantage of the concept of empowerment is a worthy endeavor that capitalizes on the investment that has already been made on the previously discussed people characteristics. Use the following questions as part of your recurring azimuth check assessment to help guide you in assessing your organization's ability to empower people and teams.

People – Azimuth Check
Empowerment
Are individual position roles and goals captured in a manner that assigns responsibility and leadership opportunities?
Are teams or COPs/COIs created and formalized in some fashion with a mechanism that communicates the team purpose and supporting roles and goals?
Are "best practice" templates or examples easily accessible to these teams to help them plan and execute the mission at hand?
What method is in place to review progress and hold the individuals and teams accountable for action? How frequently do these reviews take place?
Interview employees and discuss their role within these teams. Do they feel that they have been empowered with the authority to get the job done? Do they feel that honest mistakes are written off or that mistakes become the primary focus of the organization's leaders?

Conclusion

I have highlighted the key characteristics of people and how they impact the principles of the LM. These characteristics influence many other characteristics that make each of us who we are and determine how we interact within any organizational structure. Furthermore, it is the whole person who must be considered when an organization analyzes people, processes, and technology on a continual basis to improve team performance. The following table captures benefits related to leadership/ management as well as to the organization as a whole when your people approach considers the key concepts discussed in this chapter.

Following the table I use a question-driven format to elicit reflections from a guest expert related to the content of this chapter and the concepts of the overall LM. I have incorporated this technique in the remaining chapters. I hope you enjoy these reflections from guest experts who come from various backgrounds and with whom I have enjoyed a personal and professional relationship. As I stated previously, it is important to analyze situations from various perspectives and to recognize that we continually learn from the people we encounter throughout life. I believe that providing these reflections will enhance your understanding and appreciation for the content of the remaining chapters and further assist you in developing your own leadership identity.

Key concepts and benefits to you as a leader and to the organization

Trust – the foundation of every relationship

Benefits to the Leader/Manager:	Benefits to the Organization:
• Enables you to lead effectively regardless of rank or position • Provides the trustworthiness essential to your ability to shape or challenge people	• Promotes an organizational climate that values communication and openness • Promotes an environment receptive to change and continual improvement

Passion – driver to success

Benefits to the Leader/Manager:	Benefits to the Organization:
• Viewed by team members as positive and confident • A key characteristic for consideration when assigning roles and goals to the team	• Creates a high energy climate ready to meet the challenges related to continual improvement • Minimizes management oversight requirements for team members and stimulates the drive to succeed

Skill and knowledge – competency is fundamental to leadership and organizational success

Benefits to the Leader/Manager:	Benefits to the Organization:
• A continuous effort to maintain relevant knowledge creates long-term success	• Creates an organizational climate that recognizes and rewards professional development activities

Complementary – teaming people together in a synergistic manner

Benefits to the Leader/Manager:	Benefits to the Organization:
• Recognizing strengths and weaknesses enables powerful team building • Understand an individual's passion, knowledge and skill when you assign roles and goals	• Creates a team atmosphere where people are quick to assist each other • Positioning people to succeed creates a synergy for success

Empowerment – the final step to building a strong team

Benefits to the Leader/Manager:	Benefits to the Organization:
• Presents opportunities for you to learn from the people you have empowered • Turning over the reins to others is the true representation of your ability to lead	• Grows a strong bench of leaders who can be called on as needed to support the organization • Creates a climate that attracts and retains high caliber performers who are looking for challenges

People — A Key to Solution Success

Our first guest expert is Jim McCarthy. Jim is the CEO of Key Solutions, Inc. (KSI). KSI provides consulting services to federal contractors. These services include performing market assessments, providing advice on how to win contracts, assessing a contractor's performance, helping to prepare government bids and proposals, and furnishing technical writing services.

KSI helps its clients win or retain Government contracts by providing the "key to winning." The company specializes in helping companies (both large and small) enter the U.S. Government contracts market or increase their market shares. For the past 26 years, KSI has supported more than 300 clients doing business, or seeking to do business, with the U.S. Government. The company serves a third of the Top 100 Federal Contractors as published by *Washington Technology* in 2009. Two dozen of its clients are listed as members of the *Fortune 500*. Since 1983, KSI has played a role in clients winning over $100 billion in Federal contracts.

Jim's career spans 26 years of marketing and proposal development support in the Government contracts arena. As CEO and founder of KSI, his leadership has forged a people-focused organization that seeks to be the first consulting firm of its kind that a senior executive turns to when faced with a "must win" Government contract opportunity, or when failure is not an option.

I have worked with Jim on various initiatives since retiring from the Army in 2005 and have first-hand experience with many of his innovative ideas related to "Principle-Centered Winning,"™ the KSI Advantage™ Proposal Process (a disciplined, yet customizable approach to delivering the key to winning contracts for clients) and KSI's Business Development Toolbox™ (a collection of proven best practices that help win Government contracts). Jim's experience operating KSI, as well as the consulting services he provides to other companies, made him an obvious choice as a guest expert to provide his thoughts on people and how to successfully bring them into a team. Now for his thoughts related to this chapter, the principles of the LM and the questions that I pose. Enjoy his insights.

Q. Please provide your thoughts on how your people and the three individual characteristics (trust, passion, and knowledge/skill) identified previously in this book have established a foundation of success for KSI.

KSI's clients perform projects of critical national importance. Our clients protect our nation and combat terrorism. They fight cancer and improve the health of all Americans. They battle crime. They clean up the environment and reduce waste. They develop alternative sources of energy. They enable the federal courts to administer justice and ensure the right to speedy trials. They even search for the origins of the universe.

Our clients— **their people**— do all of these things and more. But first they must win the contract. That is where **our people** shine and we are honored to help. Our work matters.

Q. How do you define success?

I define success as helping our clients win the right work, at the right time, in the right way, and achieve the right, winning results. We call this "Principle-Centered Winning"^{TM} (PCW). For our people, PCW is a different way of thinking, conducting business, and creating value for our clients. PCW is focused on winning— but winning the right way, not just any way. PCW is a code of conduct, a set of ethical principles. PCW is based on service, sacrifice where necessary, and always acting in the paramount interests of our clients. PCW is a challenge to conventional business wisdom. I have found that to focus solely on profit and exclusively on what is in **our** best interests will cause us to lose our ethical compass, or as this book describes it, turn wrongly from our Leadership Map. But, if we focus on what is good for our clients, then business will naturally come to us. We will not only endure, we will prosper.

Q. Why is trust so important to your company?

Because ours is an extremely tough business. Unfortunately, for some, winning is all that matters. Regrettably, in our line of work, there is usually only one winner. Unlike the Olympics, those who fail to come in first are not comforted by silver or bronze medals. Moral victories do not count. No executive wants a second or third place finish.

Where millions are spent, often in pursuit of billion dollar contracts, the margins of victory are slight. With the stakes so high, so is the potential to divert from the correct path. Left to its own devices, our industry fosters unhealthy competition, unleashes enormous egos, creates climates of cynicism, and spawns suspicion and distrust— all in the name of, or perhaps because of— the fanatical pursuit of winning at any cost. So Ed is absolutely correct. People are the key to success. And because this is so, fostering, deserving, giving, and receiving trust must be prime goals for any who aspire to the burden of leadership.

Q. How is trust manifested at KSI?

Trust manifests itself each time a client calls upon us to help it win contracts worth millions, hundreds of millions, or even billions of dollars. Part of the trust factor is imbedded in our very business model. We operate with no layers of intervening overhead. As CEO, I delegate full authority commensurate with the responsibility and accountability. I avoid micromanaging Engagement Directors. This freedom from interference is an indication of trust by the company. Time after time I marvel how a trusted, passionate, and empowered team will overcome any obstacles, if only I give them enough room to operate. I am honored that our people consistently respond to this grant of trust by delivering on all their commitments— by keeping their word and meeting their deadlines through high quality work. Sometimes it takes courage to let people find their own path— maybe even fail, if that is the right term. But trust begets trust. People live up to the company's expectations and our clients are the direct beneficiaries of this climate of trust.

Q. You mentioned the passion of your people. How do you define passion and what are the keys to attaining it at your company?

Passion is enthusiasm to deliver our client the absolute key to winning. Others define passion as placing the clients' interests first. Some are passionate about making our client the hero to his or her company. There are those who are passionate about delivering exceptional value on every work product and exceeding a client's expectations. More concretely, our employees exhibit passion by going above and beyond the call of duty— working 60-hour weeks, sacrificing weekends and forgoing holidays or vacations, working extended duty assignments away from home, being on-call 24/7, and pulling all-nighters to get a proposal out the door.

There are many keys to summoning passion. First, the work must be seen as intrinsically important and that makes a difference to our clients and to the nation. A clear mission and corporate vision are paramount. So are a set of guiding principles around which all can rally. A proper delegation of authority certainly helps. Building a sense of team contributes to passion. Modeling humility and respect also are vital. Expecting the best from employees— and holding them accountable to this very high standard— also are key. But in the end, one can't *make* people passionate. One can only *become* passionate. In the end, servant leadership— seemingly a walking contradiction— unlocks the very essence of passion in people.

Q. How has the knowledge and skill of your people contributed to estab-

lishing a foundation of success for KSI?

Let me make it clear: without the knowledge and skill of our people there would be no KSI. Regarding knowledge, we aspire to create an environment of continuous learning and improvement. Candidly, we have come a long way, but there is yet much to do. The types of knowledge we need to be successful are varied. They include: an appreciation for our proposal methodology and toolbox; a comprehensive understanding of the Government procurement process; a sufficient insight into our client's business practices, as well as those of our client's customer; a healthy awareness of our competitors and our client's competitors; and if not possessing domain subject knowledge expertise ourselves, we at least need to know where to find and access it.

To improve the knowledge quotient of our employees and company, we hire the highly educated. We routinely retain the services of industry veterans and subject matter experts who have already surmounted our industry's rather steep knowledge learning curve. We codified our proposal processes and toolbox and now offer in-house training with appropriate courseware and manuals. We dispatch our people to professional development workshops and seminars. Recently, we embarked on a promising internship program to place new hires in the field under the mentorship of a veteran. We have tailored a variety of commercially available knowledge data bases to monitor and analyze future contract opportunities.

We also made significant investments in technology. Now, in one central repository, we have a secure online capability to increase staff communications/collaboration, manage corporate engagement data, and improve our business workflow. Our homepage provides employees with information on current events, announcements, staff contacts, and navigation to our corporate calendar. Our Data Center contains company information, policy and procedures, staff resumes, and other reusable content. An engagement management module provides information on engagements and assigned staff for planning purposes. A client projects database tracks client activity and the contract opportunities that are important to them. Our Associates database contains credentials and data for more than 200 consultants we use from time to time. Knowledge *per se* is not a problem for us. It is the management of that knowledge that presents us with ongoing challenges.

Regarding skills as an element of the people equation, once again I am in total agreement with my colleague, Ed. As he so persuasively sets forth in this book, there is indeed a difference between knowledge and skill. Both are important, but the terms are not interchangeable. This distinction is even more meaningful as it applies to our company.

The skills we require also are varied in nature, but I doubt they can be learned in the classroom. Our people require a vast array of interpersonal skills, poise, and even grace to operate in a high-stakes "fishbowl" of visibility. They must be able to prosper, not just cope, with severely constrained resources or with insufficient or barely sufficient budgets. They must be determined enough to meet the Government's non-negotiable and tight deadlines. They must be confident, and yet humble enough to make recommendations and decisions in the face of less than perfect knowledge. Yet they must also be flexible enough to maneuver through an environment often characterized as political or otherwise containing unknown agendas.

When I counsel members of our team I advise them to work on certain skill sets that are never learned through text books. I tell them to be bold. Be confident. Be committed to winning— but winning the right way. I recommend that they become skilled in listening well. I recommend that they always simplify complex concepts. I tell them, in the best interests of our clients, to stake out a position or make a recommendation, defend it with passion, and yet know when to be flexible and open to competing views and positions. I urge them to communicate effectively. Write well. Be patient and forgiving. Share the credit with others or even deflect it to the team as a whole. Stay focused. Lastly, I advise them to integrate their work products seamlessly with the work products of others— and, by all means, check their egos at the door and forswear pride of authorship.

Q. Consider and elaborate on these three characteristics (trust, passion, and knowledge/skill) in terms of recruiting, training, and retention.

It is a two-way street, of course, but trust must be earned every day. Perhaps, trust can be instilled. But more often, trust is conferred. It is first something one earns. Under the right conditions, passion can be nurtured. But it, too, is fragile and may be extinguished virtually overnight. Knowledge and skill must be carefully mixed to create a blend in which all parties (employees, company, and clients) mutually benefit.

But the juxtaposition of trust, passion, knowledge, and skill— often sought but so rarely achieved— creates a virtually unstoppable force. Call that force chemistry, charisma, team work, power, know-how, market presence, or leadership. Although it may not be readily defined, this force can be recognized easily. We call the offspring of these qualities success. By no means do I imply that my company has achieved this lofty stature. Fortunate is the leader-executive that contributes to the singularly rare combination of characteristics described in this book.

Q. With an awareness of this foundation of your people, please elaborate on how you employ your team members in a complementary manner based on their individual strengths and weaknesses.

We employ our team members to strengthen the team and compensate for individual weaknesses. We call this technique our Integrated Task Team Model. Because our people are foundational to our success, we value and safeguard them as the crown jewels of the enterprise. Our rough and tumble, high-stakes business imposes on us the burden to prevent employee burnout. We deliberately vary the nature and extent of assignments. We also frequently change the responsibilities and authorities of staff assigned to any project. Assignments are therefore based on a team member's individual strengths and weaknesses, as well as the client's need.

One way to do this is to create constantly changing Integrated Task Teams that form around a specific project. Each multi-disciplinary team serves under the direction of a different Engagement Director, a trustworthy person most equipped to implement our concept of Principle-Centered Winning. Sometimes he or she is a senior officer of our company. But frequently lead assignments are delegated to the person with an exceptional skill set and whom we trust most to act on behalf of our client. On those occasions, all staff— even the CEO— reports to the Engagement Director. Once the assignment is complete, Integrated Task Teams then disband only to form again in a slightly different configuration for the next project.

Creating an Integrated Task Team provides the structure for achieving complementary assignments and skills. But the structure itself does not guarantee that team members will work effectively as a team. To help ensure effective team work, we advocate a proven set of principles:

Insist on team work and cooperation. Give it. Expect it. Receive it.

Stand for something good and important. By definition, the work our client is pursuing is intrinsically important. Now you and your team go figure out a way to win it for them.

Be bold. The client is not hiring our team to be timid, nor to trot out the same timeworn solutions. Innovate.

Be different from our competitors. In a positive way, of course. Let your team's chemistry speak volumes about who you are.

Meet a compelling need and a higher purpose. This could be different for each person. Only you can figure out what that purpose is. Just don't settle for the mundane. There is nothing more powerful than a team working in the same direction.

Stretch ourselves and others in pursuit of important objectives. Challenge yourself and your team to excel.

Model an extraordinary commitment. Make it so your team is more committed to the clients' success than they are. Each team member should make this their personal priority.

Exceed our client's expectations by going the extra mile. This is the best way for your team to be invited back.

Be a good steward of the assets of our clients. Your team should safeguard the assets (including the client's brand) as if you own them.

Hold ourselves accountable and meet our commitments. This will separate your team from 90% of everybody else. Never go back on your word.

Apply these principles always— especially when it is not convenient or easy. The test for your team comes most during the dark days. Anyone can act right when the sun is shining.

Q. Please discuss how you then empower them as a team to perform the tasks.

Empowerment of our team is critically important. Empowerment is only effective if it is rational, credible, proportionate to the task, unambiguous, communicated clearly, and understood fully. Here are the methods we employ to ensure the Engagement Director and his or her team is empowered to perform any task.

Appoint a Leader. Someone qualified and trusted. Don't just give him or her the responsibility to lead, but also the authority. Then stand behind your decision. Do not waffle.

Create an Integrated Task Team. Using the model described earlier, create a team that optimizes the individual skills of its members. Make sure they are motivated.

Explain the Desired Outcome. State the objective or outcome. For us, most often it is win one for our client. Just to be sure, put it in writing.

Provide a Written Statement of Work or Task Statement. Articulate the mission. Delineate the activities and tasks. List what deliverables should emerge from the team.

Negotiate a Budget and Level of Effort. Make sure the client knows how much he or she is paying, and for what. Then be sure to share this with the team leader, if not the entire team.

Define a Schedule. It is impossible for your team to deliver on time if it is in the dark about milestones. Making the schedule aggressive is okay. But also make sure it is achievable.

Provide a Team Organization Chart. Everybody on the team should see themselves on the organizational chart. Furthermore, they must know unequivocally to whom they report. No gray areas.

Create Position Descriptions. The list does not have to be long. But let each person know in writing his or her duties, responsibilities, and authorities. Then hold them accountable.

Equip Your People with the Processes and Technologies to Perform. We call it our KSI Toolbox— everything needed to do the job. It includes work packages (roadmaps to completion) and processes. It also includes technology. You probably call it something else.

Commit Your Strategy to Writing. If necessary, employ the services of a professional facilitator to help craft your strategy. Define what you are offering that will make a difference to the ultimate decision maker.

When these items are in place, it is a good bet that your team is empowered and knows it. Miss too many of these items, and you are sowing the seeds for disaster.

Q. Please share some of your thoughts on how to build off the characteristics in this book to improve the company and individuals within the company.

I am excited about Ed's concept of a Leadership Map. With his framework in mind, I offer my own complementary leadership concepts.

Exercise Authority and Responsibility. Authority can be delegated. It also can be avoided— but only at the gravest risk. Responsibility cannot be delegated. Not if you wish to be a leader. Exercise authority and accept responsibility wisely.

Set an Example. Every company needs a role model. Every company needs a leader. As Ed has said, you be that leader.

Listen No Matter What. If you are to honor your team, reinforce its trust, summon its passion, and leverage its knowledge and skills, you have no choice. You MUST listen. Stop deceiving yourself and recognize that you are not the source of all wisdom.

Set the Vision and Communicate It. This is first on a long list of things you owe your team. This cannot be delegated. It cannot be fuzzed. You must possess an unquenchable vision and communicate it. Then communicate it 10 more times.

Share the Credit. Better yet, deflect it to your team. They deserve it. You can bask in the afterglow of a job well done, but only after you humble yourself to realize that were it not for your team, you would be nowhere.

Accept the Blame. This is the converse of the principle just above. When something goes wrong, claim the blame. After all, you are responsible. No finger pointing unless you point your own finger at yourself. Your team will respect you for it.

Exceed Expectations. Easy to say perhaps. Harder to do. But this one quality alone will make your team stand out from the pack. Your clients will love you for it.

Take Care of Your People. Frankly, if you can't do this, you are in the wrong job. Do yourself and your team a favor and step down now. Before anyone gets hurt.

Q. Finally, as you look back in your professional and personal life, share any final thoughts you have related to leadership/management and the impact it has had on your life.

Thank you, Ed. Thank you for the generosity to give me a platform to talk once more about a subject near and dear to my heart. From reading this chapter it will not surprise you if I mount my soap box once more to espouse the virtues of PCW. "Winning" in your case may not mean being awarded a contract. In your case it may mean "winning" in life or at home or at school. These same principles can be applied to anyone who dares to step forward to a position of leadership. I share these with you and your readers.

Some Tenets of Principle — Centered Winning

1. **Your Focus**: Be client-focused, not internally focused. No matter the activity, your mission is to serve the client, and each other.
2. **Your Key to Success**: To succeed, put the interests of your customer or client first. Then think of your interests and those of your company.
3. **Your Mission**: Your mission is to serve and sacrifice, if necessary, for your clients. Not profit. Profit and prosperity will automatically flow if you keep this in mind.
4. **Your Supercharged Effort**: Go Beyond the Minimum. Help your client think about what extraordinary features and qualities of his or her company actually make a difference in the world.
5. **Your Humility**: Remember: It is not about ME, YOU, or your company. It is about your clients.
6. **Your Purpose**: Not one of you is at your company by accident. Re-

flect on this and what it means. You have a higher purpose. Your responsibility, unless you already know it, is to discover what it is and how it will benefit your clients and your company.

7. **Your Sense of Fair Play**: You will engage in no transaction (deal, project, or undertaking) which does not benefit all who participate in it.
8. **Your Burden**: Lead by example, not by words. Enough said.
9. **Your Mindset**: Think of Principle Centered Winning as a way of giving back for all the good that has happened in your life.
10. **Your Invitation**: Join us. Think about these principles. Incorporate them in what you do. Live them. Pass them on.

Ed's Final Thoughts

Before we look at process and the specific characteristics related to the LM, it may be helpful for you to pause and think through the material that was presented in this chapter. Everything you do in life will ultimately come down to your ability to deal with people. In Chapters 6-8 this reality will be communicated in various manners and from many perspectives. Jim has provided great insight based on his experience running an extremely successful company that has stood the test of time. The LM is all about finding your leadership identity and continually enhancing what works for you. Jim presents material that complements my thoughts on people and how important it is for a leader to recognize that their people are the key ingredient to success. Now is a great time for you to jot down your thoughts related to people and the characteristics or principles or tenets that you feel are important from an individual basis and for the team environment.

Chapter 4

Process — Finding the Right Balance

This life is a process of learning.
- Lauryn Hill

Life itself is a process. When you think in terms of processes you will find that everything has a process to it, whether you are talking about the process involved in breathing or a process an organization uses to develop people or sell a product. In this chapter, we will cover three basic characteristics of processes that can be used to help your organization implement the best processes to support the uniqueness of their particular situation. The LM is itself a process approach to enhancing organizational efficiency and effectiveness by monitoring and adjusting the relationship among people, processes, and technology. As you study the LM you will see that it is a simple and focused approach that is standardized and repeatable yet still adaptable to the uniqueness of any situation. The LM is a great example of what you want from every process that you have in place. In fact, you can take the LM model and use it as a guide for any process or sub-process within an organization.

The LM is designed to balance three basic process characteristics that you and your organization should strive to achieve: Simple and focused, standardized and repeatable, and adaptable.

Simple and Focused

My thoughts before a big race are usually pretty simple. I tell myself: Get out of the blocks, run your race, stay relaxed. If you run your race, you'll win...channel your energy. Focus. - Carl Lewis

This first characteristic is sometimes the most overlooked when it comes to an organization putting processes in place. A simple and focused process should involve the fewest people within the process as well as the most appropriate technology. Most importantly, the process should be focused on accomplishing the desired result. The more complex the process and the more people involved, the less likely it will be successful. By keeping it as simple and focused as possible the process is timely, which is important when it comes to overall effectiveness. We are always looking for ways to simplify our lives. From a business perspective we want to do business with people who make it easy for us. For example, there are two gas stations near my house. One has the ability to take my credit card at the pump and the other does not, meaning that I must walk into the store to purchase gas. I always go to the station with the card reader at the pump. This very simple example demonstrates how one small change in a process was enabled by technology to make it more convenient for customers to do business with this gas station. Similarly, consider the convenience that online banking provides customers versus the traditional approach of going to local branch offices. Again, the process has been simplified yet remains focused on accomplishing the same result.

One way to help streamline a process is to look at it in relationship to other processes within an organization, or an enterprise, to identify duplication of effort. Often energy is expended to obtain information that already existed in other areas within an enterprise. An example of this with which almost everyone can identify is personnel information.

Personnel information is normally needed by almost every other functional division within an organization. Individuals often are forced to rewrite their name, social security number, address, phone number, and other personal information over and over again within the same organization.

> **One way to help streamline a process is to look at it in relationship to other processes within an organization, or an enterprise, to identify duplication of effort.**

Many of the more advanced organizations have made great strides in eliminating this obvious duplication of effort but there is still much more that can be done to take out unnecessary steps that are essentially problem areas waiting to happen. Speed and accuracy of information are two of the most obvious concerns when you have 20 people collecting the same information on any one person. What happens when the truth changes; do you think the information gets updated at all 20 locations?

One of many examples of duplicating energy on personnel information that I have been exposed to over and over again is the process involved in getting a network account established within an organization. I worked with one particular organization that had a process that was well intended to make sure that appropriate information was available on each account holder as well as to make sure that accounts were not being created for people who were not authorized accounts. However, the formal process was often very slow. Furthermore, most of the information that was required on the form they wanted filled out was already available in the HR Directorate, further frustrating many users. Ultimately, getting a network account required the coordination among a half dozen directorates within this organization before the office responsible for creating the account did so. This process left a new member of the organization frustrated, as well as limited in the ability to perform their job for up to two to three weeks. This is not the ideal way to bring a new member of your team on board.

This ineffective system was all too often circumvented in the name of speed and effectiveness. No leader or manager is ever comfortable with a team member sitting idle for weeks at a time without putting them to good use. Ideally, new members of the organization would go through an orientation process for them to learn more about the organization and their role within the organization before being put to work. During that orientation period, network accounts and other "in-processing tasks" can take place. However, in this particular situation that was not the case. If your office mates knew the right people it was not uncommon to just call the person who was responsible for creating accounts and have him create an account for the new individual in minutes. This also was common practice for the more senior individuals who processed into the organization. Although this was effective on the surface, it created either vacuums of information for other people who needed it or additional work for individuals who now tried to go back and obtain the required information they needed to maintain it on file.

If you want to simplify the process the first step is to keep the purpose in mind. Keep the process focused on the intended results. Identifying the information requirements and the authoritative source for the information is a way to streamline a process so that you are able to take advantage of information already available. In the scenario above, the HR section would be the authoritative source for personnel information and all the HR information required to establish a network account would be provided (hopefully in an automated way) to the individuals who are responsible for establishing a network account. In fact, the most efficient way to get these accounts established may be to have the entire process done by the personnel section in conjunction with in-processing, as opposed to making it a separate process all together.

As technology advances so do the opportunities to refine processes. Earlier we mentioned card readers and online banking as examples where processes were streamlined while maintaining a focus on the processes' intended purpose. Think about how software applications on computers continually become more user friendly. Word processing and creating graphics and spreadsheets quickly come to mind. The ability to communicate has been made easier with email or web applications for social networking. With these in mind, most of us have recognized the value of a calendar. Keeping a calendar for an individual is not too complex a task. The complexity comes when you want to keep a calendar for many people and the organization as a whole. In the past the solution has always been to keep several different calendars and move information from one to the other as needed to maintain an appropriate level of accuracy. This can be a lot of work for whoever is trying to maintain these calendars. Depending on the size of your organization, there are different solutions that can ease the administrative burden of maintaining different types of calendars. Google Calendar is great for smaller organizations. SharePoint provides another alternative for larger organizations.

In conjunction with the KM effort that I mentioned previously, we worked hard on getting a calendaring capability that could accomplish the intended purposes in a more streamlined manner. The challenge was to be able to capture personal events and business events on a calendar and maintain visibility on a need-to-know basis. We eventually succeeded in creating an interface between a web calendar capability and individual outlook calendars. This enabled input on the web calendar to update the individual's calendar if appropriate. The web calendar now provided an all-encompassing organizational calendar that could be sorted or filtered. Additionally, the web calendar provided information to individual users based on their roles; not all events were visible to all users. This is significant for protecting guarded or classified information based on a need to know, but it also limits irrelevant information to individual users. This approach provides a better user experience by eliminating irrelevant information.

Part of my job was to communicate to our customers these types of initiatives to get their input and hopefully make them part of the team to produce the solution. Initially, the staff could not see how this new calendar capability would benefit them. It was not until we identified the focus or purposes of each calendar and compared the individual steps associated with the old way of doing business and how the new approach could simplify their lives that we got users on board.

What can an organization do to keep processes simple and focused? It starts with reviewing processes looking for improvements (principle 2). Then, in the spirit of the third principle remember that when people or technology change, it is an opportunity to simplify and focus processes. The LM itself is an example of a simplified and focused process for the purpose of enhancing efficiency and effectiveness of an organization. Process reviews are inherent when the LM is used as the baseline for how you conduct business. The azimuth check assessments can be performed in conjunction with changes in people or technology but they also can be a scheduled event that takes place on a recurring basis, as we talked about in association with the LM concept. The process review may be the stimulus for change. Within these recurring reviews the following questions can help you assess how simple and focused a process is toward the intended purpose.

Process – Azimuth Check

Simple and Focused

	Is the overall purpose of the process clearly defined?
	Are the steps within the process logical in nature?
	How does each step support the overall intended purpose of the process?
	Are there any steps in which the information required could be obtained automatically from another area?
	During the time since the last review are there any questions or steps that have been repeatedly left out or not performed? Why?
	Have any data or information gaps been identified by anyone involved in the process?

Standardized and Repeatable

Repetition makes reputation and reputation makes customers. - Elizabeth Arden

Standardization is an important characteristic when the intent is to always have the same result at the end of the process. Standardization is closely aligned with repeatability but when I look at repeatability I am more focused on results. A standardized process may not achieve the same results if all the contributing factors cannot be replicated. For example, consider the environmental factors as well as individual's knowledge and skill, which all contribute to the end results. The ability to limit the number of factors over which you do not have control will enhance the accuracy of the results you achieve, making those results more likely to be repeated consistently. Franchise businesses rely heavily on standardization of processes for success. The intent is to put processes in place that can be successfully repeated to achieve the same results over and over again. To increase the likelihood of achieving those results, often the franchise goes beyond standardizing processes to include using standard facility layouts and the same make and model of equipment (or technology) to serve their customers. Likewise, the personnel are trained using the same technique, further limiting the potential for varied results. This approach is most obvious in the fast food industry but is not limited to that setting.

The benefit of standardizing a process is that it lessens the impact of an individual's lack of knowledge. However, that standardization also lessens opportunities for creativity. Very stringent processes are best for lower end tasks that are performed by many different people when the intent is to achieve the same end result. Another area where a strict standardized approach is beneficial is when room for error is very small. Think about flying an aircraft or operating a weapon system. For example, pilots, no matter how experienced, have a pre-flight checklist that is used to ensure that nothing is overlooked before taking off. Regardless of the reason for strict operational processes it is still important to look at process improvement initiatives. These improvements are best executed in a more controlled environment.

Standardization of process is important but keep in mind that determining to what extent tasks should be standardized is based on the environment. The LM is a standardized process approach to optimizing an organization's performance. Because the LM is designed to apply to any organization in any situation, it cannot be nearly as detailed as a specific process for making a hamburger at a fast food chain or providing a 20,000-mile service for a particular model automobile at a certified service center. In the latter examples the intent is to produce the same end result regardless of which franchised restaurant or certified car dealer you visit. Organizational "best practices" are fundamentally standardized practices that have repeatedly obtained the desired results. To the extent that people are involved in the process is the extent to which you can expect varied results. So despite the title "best practices," it may not be the best for your particular situation.

Spending more than 20 years in the Army, I have been surrounded by standardized processes that address every functional aspect of an organization. The military relies on standardized processes to overcome many challenges associated with a young workforce, high turnover rate, and safety concerns with dangerous equipment and situations. It is also useful to communicate performance expectations. The risks associated with day-to-day operations are very high and process helps to eliminate the chaos associated with military operations. My experience has been that standard processes are essential for any organization to perform consistently. The level of consistency in achieving the desired results is where people and technology both influence the success of a process. I'll discuss this further in the next section, where we'll dive into adaptability in more detail.

I have been fortunate enough to coach youth sports for my son and my daughter. I am by no stretch of the imagination a hall-of-fame

> **Standardization of process is important but keep in mind that to what extent tasks should be standardized is based on the environment.**

caliber coach but I do my best to provide each team member with a learning experience that enhances their understanding of the game in terms of each position and the bigger organizational mission. Because I have done this for some time, I have developed a standard approach to both coaching and to the strategy on the field. In essence, I have a best practice in this regard. However, the results of my approach are not always successful if the measure is wins versus losses. In fact, my results have been from one extreme to the other using that measuring stick. My "best practice" approach has produced both undefeated seasons and winless seasons. How can a standardized approach be so successful one year and not the next? The difference is primarily in the players and their knowledge and skill level. So although I have a standard approach that has proven to be successful on occasion, it has not produced repeated success in regards to winning soccer games. Another primary contributing factor that I do not control is the other team and how they play.

Should I change my approach every year based on the talent I have? I should if winning is the overall desired result I am out to achieve. In this situation, I am dealing with youngsters and for me it is more important for them to gain an understanding of the individual tactics and team strategies that surround soccer. For this reason, I have team members play in all the positions so they can gain a deeper understanding of the game and to provide them with individual growth opportunities. This approach does not always lend itself to winning soccer games in the short term. This approach does provide individuals and the team with an opportunity to become better rounded in regards to soccer and life in general, which will pay larger dividends in the long run than winning a few extra pee wee soccer games.

Now consider the soccer example in terms of the business world. In addition to "winning" (successfully performing your organization's mission), you also need to develop your team. You cannot always subordinate the personal development of your team members to winning. As was discussed in Chapter 3, that myopic approach limits the organization and the individual in achieving their full potential. In the business setting winning is more important than in youth soccer, which makes it even more important to take advantage of a standard and repeatable approach that enables team members to grow while mitigating potential shortfalls that may affect winning. You also do not want to leave professional development to chance by having individual team members serve solely in their current position with no planned opportunity to see other aspects of your mission.

I have seen many organizations go beyond just providing training and use a stepped program that methodically exposes their employees to different roles and situations in a logical progression. This approach provides an opportunity for the employee to gain the knowledge and experience from the opportunity while mitigating the risk of failure. A sample approach would be aligned as such:

1. Expose the employee to educational material and training related to the role.
2. Let the individual act as an observer for an event or designated period of time (shadowing).
3. The employee performs in the role while he is observed by an individual (reverse shadowing).
4. The individual performs in the role for an extended period with an evaluation and feedback provided.
5. If the individual meets the performance standard, he is qualified. If he is not ready the process is repeated in some fashion.

This approach enables individuals to be exposed to the standardized process of a particular role using a graduated approach that limits the potential for problems.

The soccer example and the elevated training approach are logical and easy to execute when the tasks are primary to your organization's purpose. It becomes a little more challenging to maintain proficiency and develop deep bench strength on activities that are not recurring in nature. While I was assigned to the special operations organization I mentioned earlier, as the Support Operations Officer, I had oversight responsibilities to execute deployment activities within a short, four-hour sequence. We had to be prepared to execute this four-hour deployment sequence 24 hours a day, seven days a week, but this was not our primary responsibility. As you can imagine, the activities required were identified in a time sequential manner. The defined events started with the initial notification and went through the actual deployment of the operational force and into the After Action Review (AAR).

To ensure success, each required task was defined and responsibilities assigned to specific individuals with backup personnel identified.

Whenever we received a notification to execute this type of deployment, the entire organization immediately came to work, including individuals who may not have been assigned a specific task at that time. The importance of the mission was such that we needed to have some individuals on a ready-reserve basis to assist with unforeseen situations. Because the tasks were generally outside most individuals' daily activities and we needed to maintain proficiency, we periodically performed the sequence to ensure we could consistently achieve success. During these exercises we exposed individuals from the ready reserve to a particular role so that they could gain the knowledge and skill required in that role.

Although we repeatedly performed this deployment sequence successfully, we never stopped trying to become more proficient at the task. Within the AAR forum we always reviewed what we did well and what we needed to work on to become more proficient.

These examples illustrate that standardized and repeatable processes can be applied to any organization and function. It further illustrates that your success will be dependent on individual and team proficiency in executing the tasks associated with the process and that your role as a leader is to ensure you can successfully repeat this process, which requires you to limit or eliminate areas of risk.

How does an organization best create standardized best practices that can achieve repeated success? You must start with the end in mind. What are the results you are seeking and how do they align with your organization's overall mission? Can you measure the results and the effectiveness of the process? If you look at my coaching experience in terms of wins and losses I am an average coach at best. If you look at how each individual player and the team as a whole developed and performed over the course of the season, I am confident the children and the parents would say I am much better than average.

Developing standardized processes with the intent of repeated success for all aspects of the organization should be a high priority. As discussed in the last section, the processes should be as simple as possible, and focused on obtaining results that are in line with accomplishing the organization's mission and working toward the vision communicated by the leader. The cyclic design of the LM facilitates the development of a standard and repeatable plan that you can execute, monitor, and continually adjust for every organization or COI to which you belong. Using the following questions as part of your recurring azimuth check assessment you can monitor the effectiveness and consider how standardization and repeatability influence the effectiveness.

Process – Azimuth Check
Standardized and Repeatable

	Is the process being used by different people or groups? How many?
	Can the results of the process be measured for efficiency and/or effectiveness? How?
	Can each step within the process be measured?
	How do the results of the measurements compare to the last review of the process?
	Is each person/group using all aspects of the standard process?
	Are there differences in performance related to people or teams? If yes, investigate reasons for performance differences.

Adaptable

Adapt or perish, now as ever, is nature's inexorable imperative.
- H. G. Wells

An adaptable process is one that is flexible to change regardless of the reason. The ability to balance between standardization and adaptability is a key component to success. The LM, by design, is a framework that promotes a balance between standardizing processes and adapting those processes to factors normally related to people and technology, but also to other interdependent processes. When you look at the LM diagram consider how the relationship between leaders and managers fosters adaptation. The leader communicates the intent and managers create systems that achieve results. The results are monitored and measured. These results, coupled with opportunities to enhance production, are analyzed by the leader/management team and then feedback is provided, creating opportunities to make improvements. The recurring azimuth check assessment concept we have been discussing is a tool that will help you balance all the characteristics we have discussed related to people, processes, and technology. This concept prevents getting stuck in a rut where the checklist mentality overrides common sense. Opportunities for adaptation at the lower levels and the upper levels of the organization are lost when individuals at all levels are not engaged in looking for opportunities to change a process for the better.

The ability to adapt to unforeseen circumstances on a situational basis is another critical aspect of success. Whether the intent is long-term process adaptation or to overcome unforeseen circumstances, success is very much dependent on the people and their un-

> **The ability to balance between standardization and adaptability is a key component to success.**

derstanding of the overall intent of the process. An empowered team member can rise to the occasion to fix shortfalls that happen based on circumstances if they understand the bigger picture and an environment that promotes individual initiative is present.

I remember once checking out a video from the small library we had on our tiny camp when I was stationed in the Sinai Desert. I had left my ID at my room, but because I was near the library I wanted to check out a video to watch that night. A soldier working during his off duty time was working the check-out counter. The standard procedure was to check the ID card and document in the individual's account the date and time that he checked out a book, or in this case a video. I had been in the library often and knew my account number.

As I approached the counter, I explained who I was and that I did not have my ID but I did know my account number. He replied, "I know that you are Captain Zimmerman but I need to check your ID." I tried again to explain to him that my ID was in my room but if he looked at the last folder in his file he will see my name and the account number will match the account number that I mentioned. He looked in the file and sure enough what I said was accurate. He acknowledged that my name and account matched but explained that he needed to see my ID before he could let me have the movie.

I never got the movie that day, despite the fact that during our discussion he acknowledged the purpose of checking my ID was to establish who I was so that he could make sure the movie was checked out to the right person. This is a simple example of a checklist mentality where the individual working down the checklist does not understand why he is doing a specific task and so he is not able to adapt to unique situations that might routinely occur. We have all faced similar situations. Sometimes this is due to the individual not understanding the larger intent of the process. Sometimes situations like this are due to a climate in which somebody steps outside the "checklist" and gets ridiculed or punished. The organizational atmosphere created by the latter example makes it difficult for people to work through those challenges that frequently come up.

How do you create adaptable processes within an organization? The short answer is to promote a mindset that understands that change is required to succeed. The most effective way to create an adaptive process is to build from the first two characteristics we discussed (simple and focused, and standardized and repeatable). This foundation ensures that your process is designed to meet intended purposes and that you are able to measure the effectiveness. With measures in place you can look for improvement opportunities to adapt the process for success. Without this foundation in place, organizations often jump from one flawed process to another without being able to identify whether their change has helped or hurt. With this in mind, it makes sense that we will build upon what we have already talked about and capitalize on recurring azimuth check assessments to seek opportunities for improvement. The following questions and actions can help you in your recurring assessment.

Process – Azimuth Check
Adaptable
Review the process related to any previous adaptations made during earlier reviews. How do the results compare to previous periods?
Analyze results with appropriate personnel and determine the cause of good and bad performance difference.
Make process changes (if required) based on analysis.
Communicate process performance information and changes based on findings.

Conclusion

Successful processes maintain a balance between the characteristics that we discussed: simple and focused, standardized and repeatable, and of course adaptable to change. Each organization is unique just as every situation is unique. However, using the cyclic nature of the LM to communicate, plan, execute, and then measure the performance of a process will contribute to continual process improvement. A recurring review of your processes using the azimuth check assessment concept will enable you as a leader/manager to focus your energy appropriately in the areas that require your attention while institutionalizing accountability and continual improvement throughout the organization.

The following table captures benefits related to leadership/ management as well as to the organization as a whole when you employ the key concepts discussed in this chapter.

As we have discussed throughout this chapter successful franchised organizations have a deep appreciation for the importance of process. I have presented different examples and stories that portray how processes drive success and are interrelated to people and technology in terms of accomplishing the objective at hand. To close this chapter, I want to bring in a different perspective on the subject of processes. As I said early in the chapter, life is a process. Our body is a system made up of numerous processes. With that in mind, I have asked Dr. Mike Mathes, President of Mathes Family Chiropractic, P.C., to be the guest expert and share his reflections on this chapter and how process contributes to the success of his Family Chiropractic Practice. I think you will enjoy how Mike shares a very comprehensive view of how process influences all aspects of his practice. Before sharing Mike's answers to the questions, I want to tell you a little bit about Mike. Mike and I have known each other for more than 30 years. We went to high school and college together. Although our careers took us down different paths, we still stay in touch today sharing opinions on many personal and professional subjects. After we graduated from Radford University, Mike entered the workforce and I went into the Army. Several years later, Mike decided to pursue chiropractic. Mike was quick to open his own practice shortly after graduating from Palmer College of Chiropractic in 1997 with a Doctorate of Chiropractic. (D.C.). He has remained a student of his profession, seeking continual improvement in his chiropractic medicine and running his own business. I am sure you will enjoy his insight as he reflects on how process has contributed to his success.

Key concepts and benefits to you as a leader and to the organization

Simple and focused – the foundation to efficiency and effectiveness

Benefits to the Leader/Manager:	Benefits to the Organization:
• Enables you to guide and monitor the organizational effort and resources wisely • Provides a map to empower junior leaders with opportunities to lead	• Maximizes time and organizational resources to accomplish desired result(s) • Promotes an organizational climate that balances results with continual improvement

Standardized and repeatable – enables energy to be focused wisely

Benefits to the Leader/Manager:	Benefits to the Organization:
• Less time can be spent on daily operations and more time on strategic improvement • Lends itself to be easily measured and results analyzed for improvement	• Provides easy guide to perform daily operations while reducing the risk of errors • Best practices can be established and capitalized within other organizational areas

Adaptable – essential to overcome situations and maintain sustained results

Benefits to the Leader/Manager:	Benefits to the Organization:
• Develops leadership skills related to seeking opportunities for improvement • Capitalizes on good performance measurement to guide improvement	• Creates a climate of continual improvement through process improvement • Provides team building opportunities between all personnel involved within the process

Process — A Way of Life

Q. Please provide your thoughts on how the following three characteristics of processes (1. simple and focused, 2. standardized and repeatable, and 3. adaptable) have established a foundation of success for you and your business.

"We were created to make manifest the full expression of life... as long as there is no interference." -Anonymous

The above quote is one that our organization is not only well aware of but is the crux of our mission. Healthcare is, or should be, about identifying what is keeping an individual from reaching his or her full potential in all areas of life.

Life processes, as Ed touched on at the beginning of this chapter, are one of the greatest natural examples of process and how exceptionally well a body can function or conversely become dysfunctional, which leads to disease if the process breaks down. When there is interference to any of the body processes that interference will eventually lead to disorder and disease and inevitably a slow or rather sudden death. An organization functions in a very similar manner.

The most appropriate example of this would be of conception and the eventual process of life that follows. At conception, if the right conditions are met, a single sperm cell penetrates an egg. At that moment all other sperm cells stop trying to find and impregnate the egg and they just swim randomly until they die and are eventually expelled from the female reproductive tract. This process will repeat itself every time as long as there is no interference.

Following conception the sperm and egg become one cell and the process of life begins. This one cell divides into two identical cells and then four identical cells and so on until the next step in the process takes place, which is called differentiation. Differentiation is the process whereby the duplicating and identical cells start to line up and form what will become the brain and spinal cord and eventually the rest of the body.

Without going into the entire embryological process, it becomes evident that there is a repeatable and time-tested process that will end with the birth of a baby some 280 days later— as long as there is no interference.

What does this have to do with the topic of process in an organization? In a word, everything! One of my favorite quotes is, "If you don't know where you are going, any road will take you there." In other words, if you don't have goals and a process to help you reach those goals your organization and life will never be able to reach their full potential. Ed's model of designing your processes as simple and focused, standardized and repeatable, as well as adaptable, is self-evident in the life process.

While not a simple process by man's standards the life process is very focused, is very standardized and repeatable, and this new life process has the innate ability to adapt as conditions change. What a great business model the human body is... as long as there is no interference.

Q. With these three characteristics of process in mind how have you been able to ensure your processes and how has your business maintained efficiency and effectiveness?

Our organization is purpose-driven, which also means that we are process driven. In order to fill our unique role in the new healthcare paradigm we have developed and implemented a process for almost all aspects of the organization. From the first time the phone rings and someone seeks information about our services to how we care for patients and how we handle the complexity of working with insurance companies, we have developed a process to make us efficient and ultimately reach our goals. We are, however, a work in progress. As business climate, insurance and governmental regulations, technology, and people change so do our processes to serve our patients and our mission.

Before we begin to implement any new process in our organization, and I believe this is as important as the process itself, we must change or challenge our own and our employees' beliefs regarding what it is we are attempting to accomplish within the process. In short, we must fully believe in and understand how this process will benefit us and our clients' needs. We have learned that beliefs dictate behavior, behavior dictates results, and results confirm belief. If someone in the organization believes that a process will only make their job harder or put more work on their desk their behavior most likely will be one of resignation or resentment and the end result will only prove to them that it wouldn't work. They will even consciously or subconsciously sabotage the effort, which confirmed their belief in the first place. If we can challenge their beliefs and let them see how this process will be a great step to enhance our organization and our clients' experience, their behavior will change and results will be seen which positively confirm the belief that we presented. Their input and participation in the final development of the new process is vital in this effort. Without it, the process might eventually be fully implemented, but there will be many more roadblocks to its full and timely implementation. Only when everyone is satisfied and fully believes that the process will save time and money, and create a more positive environment for us and our clients, will we start implementation.

One example of our purpose is to provide efficient and timely patient care. I, for one, do not like to squander my time and assume that our patients feel the same way. If I have an appointment with someone and they are consistently late, I will go elsewhere for the required services. Somehow, waiting minutes to hours in appropriately named "waiting rooms" at many doctors' offices for your appointment time has become the accepted norm in healthcare. Therefore, we have developed a process of patient flow that virtually eliminates lengthy wait times when a patient is on time for their appointment.

One of our biggest challenges with regard to developing and implementing processes is that we have to remain mindful that our organization, like the human body, is vitalistic and not mechanistic. Our organization, like most organizations, is a living entity because it is run by and for people. It is constantly changing and we have to be vitalistic enough to be able to identify the challenges and then adapt positively to these challenges. Take the seemingly simple process of body temperature regulation as an example. If the environment you are in is hot, or if you are working your body in such a way that it is hot, a healthy individual will perspire, which will lower core body temperature and maintain a healthy temperature range. If an individual does not perspire under these conditions there would come a rapid onset of undesirable symptoms and if not corrected the individual will die. Adaptation is a necessary component of successful life and organizational processes.

Q. Can you discuss the importance of measuring the results of your processes and how you use these measures to improve your performance?

It is essential that our organization knows how well the various processes are working. The most obvious measurement would be financial growth but that does not tell the entire story. We have had periods of financial growth while our patient encounters actually decreased, which forced us to look at our new patient process and our recall process to make sure that they were still moving in the right direction to accomodate further growth. Like the body, each process has an effect on other aspects of our organizations; when one suffers all others suffer as well.

Q. How often do you review the processes? Please share your review process— who and what is involved?

Our organization is not driven by statistics; however, statistics are used as a measuring tool to enable us to see the bigger picture. Currently, as far as one aspect of our organizational process is concerned, we look at four major statistics: new patients, collections, patient visit average, and collections per visit. We collect these statistics daily but only review them once a month. We also look at the previous year's quarterly statistics compared to the current quarter and adapt our process if, and only if, we notice major changes in the wrong direction. As a small organization, most of our reviews involve the entire team with regard to areas that affect the entire team. If the process only involves, for example, our insurance billing department and our front desk assistant they meet and provide solutions if necessary to adapt the process to fit the situation. Once again, there will always be exceptions that do not fit a process perfectly and we give our team members the ability to work outside the process guidelines as long as it still serves our mission.

Q. Finally, as you look back in your professional and personal life, share any final thoughts you have related to leadership/management and the impact it has had on your life.

I have found through the years that being a leader of an organization and a team can be a very challenging and humbling experience. Part of our mission as a healthcare business is to do whatever it takes to do what is right by our team members and patients. While this seems to be a rather obvious part of any organization it is not always the thing that is practiced. Something as seemingly simple as forgetting to bring in paychecks on time can have a profound impact on a team member's attitude of how you, as their employer, feel about them. Thankfully I have only twice driven paychecks out to a team member's residence late at night so that they would have their checks on time. They deserve to be paid for their energy and commitment and if they aren't worth the trip it might be time to review an organization's personnel review process.

Personally calling each new patient after their first visit to our office is part of our "WOW" experience process. At first it was uncomfortable but I believed that it was essential for me to reconnect with patients to see if there were questions or concerns that they might not have thought of or were afraid to ask. I could have a team member perform this task but I believed coming from me it would have a greater impact on their healing journey. My belief dictated my behavior and the results have confirmed my beliefs many times over in this simple process; patients really appreciate it and I have found that I learn things about the patients' health condition that helps in the ultimate success in their care.

I have consistently learned that it is really the little things, if done correctly and for the right reasons, that help an organization reach and surpass its mission. When you put all the pieces together correctly the whole will be far greater than the sum of the parts. B.J Palmer, D.C., known as the "Developer of Chiropractic," was fond of saying "Get the Big Idea, all else follows." As a leader I have found that having the "Big Idea" is an absolute essential, but only if you understand that the "Big Idea" is only attainable if you know how to recognize, organize, and successfully execute all the smaller ideas while also understanding that an organization, like the human body, is a vitalistic entity that must adapt to ever-changing conditions.

Ed's Final Thoughts

As we continue our journey using the LM I think you can see how process brings order to our lives— literally. Mike has reflected on how process impacts every aspect of his business. I recommend you take some time now and do the same. Where are you falling short in meeting your goals and what process is related to that area of your life? Too many people travel aimlessly, never recognizing that to achieve success in a particular area they must first understand the underlying process involved. When I decided to write this book, I recognized that I did not know the process behind getting a book published. I had to educate myself first and ultimately I chose to solicit outside assistance as well. You may not know or care to know the details of the processes that are holding you back in obtaining your goals. That is okay, but you must recognize that if you want to achieve the goal you will either have to learn it or find someone who has the expertise to assist you in your endeavor. As we move to the next chapter consider that it may not just be someone (people) who can assist you; it also may be something (technology).

Chapter 5

Technology — The Great Enabler

The first rule of any technology used in a business is that automation applied to an efficient operation will magnify the efficiency. The second is that automation applied to an inefficient operation will magnify the inefficiency.
- Bill Gates

Like people and processes, technology plays a role in every aspect of the organization. Technological advances are what continue to enable us as a society to achieve things that could not be done by previous generations. Technology is complementary to people and processes, enabling organizations to achieve success in a more reliable and quicker fashion than ever before. Too often people do not recognize the interdependent relationship that technology has with people and process, thinking that technology by itself can remedy an organization's shortfalls. Technology can help solve the problem but if you forget about the people and the process aspects of the situations your technology implementation will become one of the many failed initiatives that fill up the tech magazines. The rapid change that technology creates is a primary reason the principles within the LM are ones that need to be managed on a continual basis. This also is the reason that when somebody says "We tried that approach before and it did not work" your question should be how long ago and what technologies were available to enable that approach.

Technology affects all functional aspects of an organization but I will focus my attention on how technology enables us to strategically move information in the most effective manner to create a knowledge-based organization (KBO). I have no intent to endorse any specific technologies that an organization should use to become better at sharing information. The truth is that technology changes rapidly and there are technologies that exist today that did not exist just a few years ago that have drastically changed the way an organization can effectively move information. The LM and this book are intended to stand the test of time and the principles of the LM are such that continual changes in people, process, and technology are required for organizations to be able to better move information and successfully perform their mission.

I have stated my passion for leadership. It has been a lifelong journey for me to continually enhance my understanding of leadership. Specifically, within the last 10 to 12 years I gained an appreciation for, or maybe even an obsession with, the importance of information or knowledge to the leader and organization and the ability, through technology, to deliver that data, information, and knowledge to decision-makers. That really is the difference between average individuals/organizations and superior ones. The transformation of my paradigm occurred while at Command and General Staff College. Shortly, I will elaborate on this more with respect to how the United States Military would completely change doctrine based on making information available to decision-makers. My roots as a logistician exposed me to the importance of data and information related to logistical functions. Within my various jobs I was continually exposed to technology in general, the reality that it is the conduit to delivering information, and that technology is always changing.

The ability to move information through an organization lets you develop knowledgeable people, which are an organization's most valuable asset. An organization has an enormous amount of data and a wealth of information. The real question is has the organization created "corporate knowledge" and, more importantly, is that knowledge being converted to wisdom by the people within the organization? Knowledge Management (KM) is achieved when people, processes, and technology are brought together in a synergistic manner so that productivity can be increased 10 fold, 100 fold, or even 1,000 fold. Technology that promotes information sharing and collaboration makes a lesson learned by one person to become a lesson learned by all. Information can move throughout the organization in a manner that lets individuals spend more time analyzing information or producing work products and less time searching for the information they need.

KM in the information age is as much of a force multiplier as the airplane was to warfare. Much like in the early days of the airplane, many people still do not truly understand just how powerful a knowledgeable worker can be. Too many organizational leaders are not able to get out of the industrial age paradigm and appreciate the new knowledge age paradigm. The organization that understands the shift of the paradigm and creates a KBO will succeed. Those organizations that don't change will become too ineffective and inefficient to compete and will become irrelevant. Leaders who use technology wisely have accurate, relative, and timely information available to them to make informed decisions.

Enabling Leaders

Failing organizations are usually over-managed and under-led.
- Warren G. Bennis

As you look at the LM, consider the role of the leader. His primary responsibility is to bring purpose and focus to the organization. The leader must be able to effectively communicate his message to guide the organization to success. The requirement to effectively communicate is a constant requirement because an organization is continually changing based on many influencing factors within and outside of the organization's control. Technology that enables leaders to maintain situation awareness and communicate adjustments based on changes in the situation is how organizations can remain relevant and successful in a rapidly changing environment.

Technology that promotes information sharing in all fashions (voice, video, and data) is critical to keeping the leader aware of current situations. Similarly, this technology can be leveraged by the leader appropriately guiding and providing feedback to his team.

In the late 1990's the Department of Defense (DOD) drastically changed its approach to warfare, an approach that primarily leveraged information superiority as opposed to superior numbers or weapon systems. I was attending the Army Command and General Staff College when the concept of information superiority was introduced in a document titled "Joint Vision 2010" (JV2010). Like many revolutionary changes, this adaptation in war fighting had many skeptics. It was a paradigm shift that many could not visualize at that time. You must understand we were less than 10 years removed from Desert Storm and Desert Shield. The "100

> **Technology that allows leaders to maintain situation awareness and communicate adjustments based on changes in the situation is how organizations can remain relevant and successful in a rapidly changing environment.**

hour" war was highly touted as the most successful display of military might in history. Why were we making such a change in approach when we were so successful? The reason was simple but maybe not fully appreciated by all watching. We needed to get better just to maintain our ability to succeed in the future. Additionally, there were inefficiencies that had an operational impact on the battlefield and financial impact on the taxpayer.

JV2010, and later JV2020, were designed to address shortfalls in all functional areas to include personnel, intelligence, operations, and logistics. The intent was to provide information systems that enabled leaders at all levels to maintain situation awareness based on accurate, timely, and relevant information that was moved appropriately to individuals who needed that information. JV2010 and JV2020 in essence said information is one of our most valuable commodities and our ability to provide it to the right people and deny it to our enemies will be the key to our success militarily. This change in doctrine has helped create many changes in technology that have impacted our nation and the world. In addition to the technology changes, there was a greater emphasis on the importance of empowering individuals up and down the chain of command with information and the authority to act upon that information. Timeliness of action based on accurate information is critical to success.

Technology that moves information up and down the chain and enables leaders to communicate direction and guidance, as well as inspire and empower more junior leaders, is valuable to any type of organization, not just the military. There is nothing more powerful than an inspired, empowered, knowledgeable team of individuals, regardless of their purpose. The use of technology to share information and work in a more collaborative manner creates an organization of leaders. As we discussed in Chapter 3, there is a synergy that is generated when a more collaborative and open approach is employed to conducting business.

With technology advances in information sharing via the Internet, individuals can lead organizations or other teams remotely by empowering a workforce that is not confined by walls and cubicles. Consider how a leader can provide vision and direction through email to a small, specified audience or to the entire organization using the company website or blog. The leader can quickly communicate to the intended audience using text, graphics, voice, or even video. The ability to communicate quickly and effectively can be done at an extremely reasonable cost. The cost of communications technology can be offset by the savings in office space, furniture, and other associated costs related to having employees work from a central office. The additional benefits associated with a telecommuter workforce will be discussed in more detail shortly, but it is safe to say that this approach provides benefits to both the organization and the individuals within. The ability to leverage technology to enable a workforce to perform in a less structured and traditional setting without a doubt requires a strong leader who is comfortable with technology.

Like every other aspect of an organization, the use of technology as an enabler should not be left to chance. A well thought-out plan can ensure technology is being used successfully to enable organizational success to include the leader's ability to communicate within the organization. Using the following questions as part of your recurring azimuth check assessment you can monitor how technology is supporting the leaders ability to communicate.

Technology – Azimuth Check

Enabling Leaders

	What technologies are available for the leader to communicate to his team?
	Is the leader comfortable with the technology? Why or why not? What can be done to correct shortfalls?
	Are team members comfortable with the technology? Why or why not? What can be done to correct shortfalls?
	Is there a communication plan for the organization that identifies what and how the leader will communicate to the team?
	Review the communications plan in conjunction with the azimuth check to ensure it is current and relevant. Does the plan align with the organization's mission, vision, and goals?

Enabling Managers

Management by objective works—if you know the objectives. Ninety percent of the time you don't. - Peter Drucker

The leader (individually or organizationally) is focused on communicating vision and direction— the results we want to achieve. The manager in us or our organization is focused on planning and executing the

> **Managers want to collect, analyze and then present meaningful information related to performance towards the mission and vision.**

tasks required for achieving the desired results. Managers primarily focus on monitoring and measuring the tasks performed within a process from an individual and team perspective. Technology plays a significant role in this aspect of the job. The ability to quickly collect data for analysis is invaluable. Managers want to collect, analyze, and then present meaningful information related to performance toward the mission and vision. This information enables the leader to then complete the loop and provide feedback and direction to the organization.

Effective managers have established performance objectives and key indicators to gauge performance. Monitoring these indicators and measuring them to established benchmarks assists managers in analyzing why objectives are not being met or how future improvements in performance may be realized. The more technology can assist with the collection of information, the more time the manager can spend doing a thorough performance analysis. Technology that is able to provide some of the analytical work is even more valuable. Much like the leader, the manager is better served when technology can eliminate some of the more cumbersome and repetitive aspects of their job.

Consider how technology supports the manager from two perspectives: (1) measuring the performance of people within the processes and (2) facilitating a process improvement in an area in which the manager is responsible. To illustrate the two perspectives consider the use of a common access card (CAC). The CAC was initially used within the Department of Defense but is now common in almost all U.S. Government agencies and is quite widespread within the private sector. CACs are used basically as ID cards with a chip that stores information specific to the card holder. Using a CAC reader (similar to an ATM card reader) as the medium to move data from the card into an application allows data to be automatically transferred as opposed to manually input. The CAC is used for many purposes, including physical access to locations and access to information within an organization's network. With a little thought it is not difficult to see how this technology can enable a manager to collect performance measures and make process improvements. Table 5-1 highlights some of the possible performance measures and process improvements that can be created using the CAC to control access to physical locations or to information.

Common Access Card Benefits. *Using CAC cards in such areas as physical access and access to information can help the organization become more efficient.*

Area	Performance Measures to Facilitate Improvements	Process Efficiencies Gained
Physical Access Control	• Accuracy of access list	• Reduce number of individuals required to maintain access control • No manpower requirement to check ID cards for access • Update access lists from a central location
	• Monitor the number of access changes performed cyclically or based on position	• Proactively make access changes based on patterns versus waiting for instruction
	• Monitor access by location to identify high-traffic areas	• Information can provide more accurate budgeting for lifecycle replacement of equipment
	• Provides history of who was in an area in case of emergency	• Reduce time and resources required to solve problems
Information Access	• Calculate overall relevance of information based on number of hits	• Push information to common sites to reduce search time for information
	• Determine what subjects are most relevant based on position	• Push information to individuals based on position (reduce time searching for information) • Ensure information is appropriate based on position (information security)
	• Monitor cyclic value of information	• Adjust presentation of information based on cyclic need (focused time and resources)

As we discussed in the process section, often technology can eliminate the need for a process altogether. A strong CAC program can eliminate the need to have ID cards manually checked. Fewer man hours will be spent monitoring and measuring access control but these activities can never be eliminated or the accuracy and confidence in your CAC program will disappear.

Let's look at another example and revisit how self-ordering technologies (text messaging, Internet, ordering kiosks) have been used to enable managers in the restaurant industry. In the last chapter we discussed how standardized and repeatable processes were essential to almost all franchised restaurants. Think what impact offering the ability to place orders using text messaging, the Internet, or a kiosk has to the customer as well as the restaurant staff and management. The capability can be implemented for both take-out orders and in-house orders. The benefits to all parties come from eliminating the "middle man" to capture the customer's order, providing more timely and accurate information.

Providing customers with this alternative means of placing orders benefits them and the staff with enhanced order accuracy and reduced order wait time. When management ensures the right people and processes complement the technology, then more long-term benefits can be realized through better use of the information. The technology makes it much easier to monitor, measure, and analyze the performance of the people and processes in relationship to performing the intended purpose. The valuable information needed for this can now be easily provided in various fashions based on specific information needs to perform trend analysis. The time saved from having to collect and organize the data can be used to create more efficient and effective solutions to problems based on your analysis. Consider how a menu change can now be communicated to everyone with a simple input into a database versus updating all the printed media.

As we have discussed in previous chapters, don't think that bringing in this technology is all that must be done. People (both staff and customers) must be trained and become comfortable with this change. A failure to recognize that you will have customers who are uncomfortable with this change will cost you customers. However, with the right people and a good change-over process you can quickly get your customers on board with the new ordering process.

Regardless of the type of organization and the business functions being performed you must determine if the technology being used to provide managers with the information needed to monitor and measure the results of the processes is in place. Using the following questions as part of your recurring azimuth check assessment you can monitor how technology is supporting the managers' need for information.

Technology – Azimuth Check
Enabling Managers

	What technologies are used to provide the manager with the information needed to monitor and measure the performance of individuals and teams?
	Is the manager comfortable with the technology? Why or why not? What can be done to correct shortfalls?
	Are team members comfortable with the technology? Why or why not? What can be done to correct shortfalls?
	What recurring reports are used by the manager to analyze performance? List reports and frequency. Identify any information gaps that exist.
	Identify any future technology implementations that are already planned. Have the manager's information requirements been identified?

Accelerator for Results

Insanity: doing the same thing over and over again and expecting different results. - Albert Einstein

Regardless of your role as a leader or manager, new technology implemented in the right manner can accelerate the organization to the desired results. The automation of redundant, cumbersome processes produces more timely and accurate results. More important, the right technology can change the way organizations share information and promote a more collaborative approach to daily business. This has a synergistic effect by creating corporate knowledge and sharing that knowledge. An organization of empowered and informed leaders (the leader within all of us) can easily be created with this type of approach. The LM provides a simple method to address people, processes, and technology that can accelerate your organization to success.

Many of the examples provided throughout this book are instances in which technology accelerated a process to obtain the desired results. I am sure that if you thought about your experiences in terms of people, processes, and technology you will agree that technology was normally used to accelerate the process toward the end result. Think about

> **Regardless of your role as a leader or manager new technology implemented in the right manner can accelerate the organization to the desired results.**

bank ATMs and self check-out registers within stores. In both cases, customers were empowered with the ability to help themselves. In return for helping themselves, they get through the process quicker. In terms of the ATM, customers may pay to get through the process faster than going into the bank to perform their transaction and most are willing to do that.

Also consider what email did to the management of information. The ability for you to send a message to the intended audience was sped up in an immeasurable way. Now consider what the Internet has done with respect to providing information to a COI. Using web services, a business can inform its workers, customers, and suppliers almost instantaneously with a change or announcement with very little human intervention. The technology can collect data, aggregate it to information, and present that information in a relevant manner for the different audiences within a COI. Revisiting a telecommuter workforce, think about the availability of this information via the Internet. The entire team is now empowered and the time saved commuting can be used more productively toward work products. The fact that your workforce can be dispersed around the country or around the world and may work from their house or a coffee shop has changed the way business can be conducted. Companies that recognize and embrace these types of changes use them to accelerate accomplishing their mission.

All of the technology changes have an initial period of learning and discomfort. It is hard for many younger people to appreciate that when email first became prevalent in the business world it was not uncommon for secretaries to print out emails and give the hard copy to the boss. The boss would then write a reply with pen on the email and the secretary would type up the reply and send it back. The more forward thinkers realized that they needed to adapt their individual knowledge, skill, and process if they were going to take advantage of this technological advancement. Leaders/managers needed to use email themselves if they wanted to stay relevant and not rely on secretaries for this function. The process of communicating was, in essence, accelerated and to survive you needed to change your process and the skills required to keep up with this technology enhancement. This type of thinking needs to be applied to today's technology and to future technology. The LM provides a solid foundation to ensure that this mindset prevails in the future. Using the following questions as part of your recurring azimuth check assessment you can monitor how well technology is helping you accelerate to your desired result.

Technology – Azimuth Check
Accelerating Results
Are the intended purposes identified for the different technologies within the organization?
Are there two or more technologies used for the same purpose? Why? Can the organization move to a single technology to accomplish the result?
Are the leaders/managers and staff comfortable with the technology? If not, why and what can be done about it?
Are there established performance objectives outside your organization so that you can benchmark your use of the technology with others in your industry? Capture them and use them to monitor your performance of the technology.
Are there any future technologies that are being implemented? What are the intended purposes? Are there established benchmarks from the old system to baseline the operation for future performance measures?

Conclusion

In this chapter we briefly highlighted the key characteristics of technology as it pertains to supporting leadership tasks and management tasks. Technology often can be viewed as an enabler that accelerates you or your organization to a desired result. Furthermore, because there are different technologies that are intended to serve the same purpose, you must evaluate your use of technology within the LM framework that considers the people and processes involved to support that function. The recurring azimuth check assessment approach is a method that provides a holistic evaluation that considers the interaction among people, processes, and technology. The following table captures benefits related to leadership/ management and to the organization as a whole when you take an approach to technology that considers the key concepts discussed in this chapter. Following the table, I have asked Pete Paradise, President of Zero Limits Solutions, to share his views with respect to how you can employ technology considering the concepts discussed in this chapter.

Key concepts and benefits to you as a leader and to the organization	
Enabling leaders – clear, concise, and timely communication creates opportunities for success	
Benefits to the Leader/Manager:	Benefits to the Organization:
• Makes communication and information sharing easy and more productive	• Promotes knowledge sharing creating a smarter workforce able to solve problems creatively
Enabling managers – accurate and timely information enables thorough analysis of performance	
Benefits to the Leader/Manager:	Benefits to the Organization:
• Provides easy access to data needed to measure individual and team performance • Supports detailed analysis for process improvement based on captured knowledge	• Upholds a climate of individual and team accountability • Allows organizations to constructively focus energy towards improvements based on knowledge
Accelerating results – a quicker journey to the same or better result is the goal	
Benefits to the Leader/Manager:	Benefits to the Organization:
• Maximizes the use of time to accomplish goals	• Creates overall efficiency for mission accomplishment

I worked with Pete Paradise on two KM efforts, one for WHCA and another for a large Navy organization with a worldwide presence. In the latter, Pete and I provided consulting services to the command with respect to developing and implementing a KM strategy that capitalized on Microsoft Office SharePoint Services (MOSS) 2007 as the technology enabler. I have known Pete and worked with him off and on for the last six years. Based on my experience with Pete, I continually seek opportunities to work with him. When it comes to implementing technology within an organization to improve collaboration and communication, I have not worked with anyone more talented than Pete. I asked him to share his thoughts with respect to how we used technology within both KM efforts. To help summarize the intent of these KM efforts, the intended purpose of the overall KM strategy we developed and implemented for the Navy command is captured below:

The Knowledge Management (KM) Strategy provides a framework to leverage KM principles to continually improve the efficiency and effectiveness of the command's daily missions. This overarching strategy capitalizes on existing improvement initiatives by focusing on improving practices and an adaptive approach to continual and methodical transformation. In addition, this strategy relies heavily on the portal, an existing KM tool, to institutionalize KM within the command. The KM efforts will use data and information to capture, store, and deliver organizational knowledge when, where, and how it is needed for all individuals within the command, in order to:

- Optimize individual and team performance throughout the command
- Improve decision-making at all levels of the command
- Create a learning organization focused on continual improvement

Technology — Upgrade Your Performance

Q. Please share your thoughts on how technology works as an enabler. Specifically, discuss how technology can enable leaders and managers, and how it can be an accelerator to bringing about change within organizations.

Ed, I truly believe when technology is embraced it is one of the most powerful weapons in the arsenal of leaders and managers to positively drive transformation within their organization. Whether your goal is to achieve optimization, improve decision-making, facilitate change, or foster innovation, leveraging technology can help you succeed in realizing a leader's vision. The ability of technology to improve a leader's capability to communicate, manage, monitor, and focus their organization in alignment with their vision is unmatched. When used correctly, technology helps leaders bring their great ideas from thought to fruition, vastly improving the chance that the organization change they seek will take hold. Technology acts to level the playing field, simplifying the dissemination, collection, and analysis of information within an organization. This is especially true within larger organizations where communications are often challenging. While smaller organizations may be able to communicate leadership concepts and orchestrate change through frequent interactions, such as reviews, status meetings, and informal touch points, etc., the ability to scale or apply those ideals to larger organizations becomes challenging and costly over time. By leveraging technology to alleviate those challenges, leaders and managers can efficiently and effectively accelerate the process of bringing about the behavior needed to be successful in their business.

Consider for a moment how effective technology is as an enabler of communications. We see it in our everyday lives, from television commercials, to text messaging, to Twitter feeds. The ability to push and pull communications across the Internet using communication devices has dramatically increased the ability to reach large audiences effectively. Leaders can, and should, leverage technology to help communicate their vision to their organization. Such technologies as streaming video, blogs, discussions boards, announcement boards, or even simply posting a strategic document to a company web site will help leaders better communicate to the masses. I have seen many organizations do this successfully. It can provide the opportunity for dispersed audiences to receive the communications at their convenience, the opportunity for staff, both current and future, to revisit the communications over time, and finally when coupled with feedback tools, such as a discussion board, can provide opportunity for dialogue among your workforce. As an example, a Navy organization I've worked with, consisting of 50,000 employees, recently went through a change of command. A new Admiral was coming on board and he had a new vision for the organization, wanting to dramatically change the way the organization performed its business. As you can imagine, the ability to reach this large and wide of an audience would be difficult. With people in different geographic locations, different time zones, and the demands of day-to-day activities, it would be near impossible to get everyone together for the Admiral to deliver a singular message that would get his staff all firing on the same vision. The Admiral recognized this and decided to leverage technology to get his message out. Leading up to the change of command he created a video that would be streamed through the organization's intranet so that all could hear his message when it was convenient to them. Upon taking command, he sent out an email to the entire organization communicating the change of command and prompting people to visit the intranet to view the video. The buzz quickly spread and people immediately began to move out toward his vision. In the weeks and months to come, he leveraged other online tools to continue the interaction, such as an idea submission tool and interactive blogs that enabled him to post information about initiatives and receive feedback from the expertise spread throughout his organization. All of these efforts resulted in greater dialogue and accelerated movement toward the leadership vision thanks to the intelligent use of technology.

Another effective way I see technology being used today by managers is to implement automated solutions that help them streamline processes, focus their staff on objectives, monitor progress toward goals, and help their divisions operate in a more turn-key manner. An added benefit of doing this is that organizations are able to better centralize knowledge created within their organization and capitalize on it for future benefit. As people come and go or move around the organization the knowledge and information they created while they were there is retained for future use and also limits the impact of organizational churn. By standardizing and centralizing around technology, managers can help to ensure that churn does not have an overt impact on operations and provides for much easier transition of responsibilities. I also have noticed that when work processes are enabled with IT, it can help managers foster competition across their organization, establish greater awareness, and drive behavior necessary to achieve goals. One way of doing this is establishing key performance indicators (KPI) and making the monitoring of those available through a company intranet so that leaders, managers, and employees alike are all focused on indicators important to the business.

You might be thinking that these types of tools require a large development staff to implement them. While that may be true in some cases, there are many tools available today that provide fairly sophisticated tools targeted at savvy end-users who can set up basic capabilities to help automate processes. An example of one such tool I've seen many organizations leverage for this is the Microsoft Office SharePoint product. When coupled with the Office Suite, SharePoint can provide enormous capability to the workforce with little to no developer intervention.

Take, for instance, if as a manager I am responsible for establishing a group of new sales teams. I want to encourage behavior in them to begin reaching out to potential clients. Our business reaches out by telephoning existing clients and potential new clients that we have gathered from several information sources. As a manager, I could decide to focus on the number of solid leads generated and leave it up to my sales team as to how they want to do that and wait until the end of the month to see how that goes. However, as the manager, I am aware that the nature of our business is a numbers game; the more contact I make, the more opportunities will come about. Actual opportunities may take several weeks, or even months, to come to a point where my organization might typically start tracking those at a higher level. Well in this case, I really want to drive the day-to-day behavior of my sales teams— I want them to spend the next few weeks tied to the telephone drumming up business for the company. In order to drive this behavior I decide to set up a mechanism to measure the number of phone calls placed by each agent and any demonstrations that have been scheduled. I generate competition amongst the teams by offering a gift certificate at the end of each week to the nicest restaurant in town to be awarded to the winner. The team that has made the most contacts after the campaign will be rewarded with an even greater prize— tickets to a local sporting event. And if my entire sales department makes a set goal at the end of the campaign, I can have some type of reward to recognize everyone. To put this plan into action I can make the tracking of this real time; as sales agents place calls or schedule demonstrations, they register that information in a simple list on our web portal. As the days go on I display a key performance indicator (KPI) for each team and each team member that everyone in the organization can see. I encourage leadership to monitor that KPI as it is eliciting behavior that we value in our organization. I request that as they pass members of the sales teams they make comments to them about the current status of the indicator and encourage the employees to go for the win.

If my assumption was correct, the more contact made with potential clients through this friendly competition will result in a greater number of solid leads in the future. Furthermore, I've begun to better institutionalize a desired behavior within the organization. And as a manager, I now have greater information to analyze, because by now tracking the volume, frequency, and other details of contacts made to clients I can begin to better understand the relationship of contacts vs. sales and better forecast future efforts. The additional information also may help me identify areas where some individuals or teams may need additional training as their numbers do not equate to those of other teams. The key here is that I've focused on eliciting a behavior that, as a manager, I believe will result in positive impacts for the organization. I'm still concerned with the final number of sales. However, because that goal is somewhat lofty, and isn't as dynamic as contact made with potential clients, by keeping the competition healthy and reflective of desired behavior, the long term effect of that behavior should be a positive for the organization.

Another frequent use of technology I see today is as an enabler to a more collaborative and open culture within organizations. Many organizations have moved toward this by establishing web portals for use by employees, customers, and partners to collaborate on their work together. These collaborative tools include such capabilities as document collaboration, discussions boards, blogs, wikis, and task lists, among other things. When done effectively, this type of environment can provide opportunities for greater participation, awareness, and opportunities for innovation as it provides one more avenue for an organization to collect information and enhance the sense of community within the workplace. One major benefit of working this way is that there is greater transparency and it improves the organization's ability to retain knowledge over time.

If your organization isn't enabling its business with technology, you should start doing so soon, as the efficiencies created by it can be truly amazing.

Q. Please share some of the challenges one might encounter when bringing technology into an organization and what are actions you find useful to take in overcoming them? For example, what people or process issues might one encounter and how do you overcome them?

Ed poses a great question here, and one we should all keep in mind when undertaking any change initiative. When it comes down to it, that's what we're doing when we're implementing new technology, implementing a change within the organization. That change, no matter how small, will impact the people and processes already existing within your organization. Implementing the technology is usually the easiest part of the change process; navigating the organizational challenges presented by it is almost always the most difficult and unpredictable aspect. If change is not managed well, it brings a tremendous amount of risk to implementing the change your desire. In my career I've identified several challenges encountered while transforming organizations through the application of technology. These challenges, if not addressed, can certainly slow, if not bring to a screeching halt, any IT innovation efforts within the organization. While the list is not exhaustive, as I sit here today, these are the challenges I think are important to be aware of and steps I believe an organization can take to mitigate them to ensure greater success of IT initiatives.

Challenge 1: Balancing People, Processes, and Technology

As Ed has woven throughout his writing, achieving results is dependent on striking a balance among people, process, and technology. This balance is especially critical when implementing technology, for without balance you are doomed for failure. As a leader, manager, or decision-maker, you must think of your people, their tendencies, their experiences, their comfort zones, and the influence these things have on implementing new processes and technologies. You must be able to understand the processes that will make your business successful, turn-key, systematic, and repeatable. On top of that, you need to be able to bring in the right technology mix that enables you to effectively guide your people, both current and future, through those processes that will help your organization operate as you have envisioned it. This is a difficult balance to strike, especially when working with a diverse workforce in a world of constantly evolving technology.

Many organizations acknowledge the workforce is in a transitioning phase, one in which many of the senior members are accustomed to running business in a more manual way based on standard operating procedures and other formal documentation, and a junior workforce that is very much used to performing activities in a more automated fashion without needing to know all the details of the process, the policies, and the procedures. I believe this to generally be true and I predict that this diversity in technology experience will continue to exist as technology is constantly evolving from year to year, meaning that my technology experience could be vastly different from those just ten years younger than myself. I also predict that people's attention to detail will continue to decline as we become more and more accustomed to needing not to know them in other parts of our lives. We are already seeing this today, as I often hear senior members of the workforce advocating strong policy and procedures to right the ship, often in a place where you can't get people to read anything longer than a page because they have become accustomed to the convenience of technology. They think about when written policy could be released and the organization would change because that policy would be enforced across the organization. This can still work today; however, it requires strong leadership, accountability, and responsibility throughout the organization— which if it is lacking at any level will result in variations.

On the other hand, I hear junior members of the workforce desiring social network type environments and online banking type experiences, without much regard for policy/procedure. They seek the ease that they've become familiar with in the Internet age and are reluctant to dive deeply into the details that the senior workforce is comfortable with doing. I see good-intentioned leaders trying to bring these whiz-bang social networking tools to their employees, often without thinking about how that capability contributes to meeting the goals of the organization. So what's the right answer— detailed policy and procedure, or free flowing social networking tools? Well, as always, the answer is somewhere in the middle. Automation is essential; however, it must be based on sound policy and procedures, and you must understand and have those documented before you pursue implementing technology. Additionally, the technology should blend well with your employees and their experiences with tools available to them in other aspects of their lives.

But I can't stress enough the need to first focus on policy and procedure before embarking on technology to facilitate it. Not doing so is to our detriment— we must start off the traditional way of defining and implementing sound procedures and then seek out modern technology that supports the business practices that will make your business successful. By doing this we obtain the best of both worlds while minimizing risk of organizational deficiencies that may exist. Furthermore, we need to ensure that our efforts are not just to keep up with the trends for the sake of keeping up, but that technology has a well-defined strategy and purpose that contributes to the long-term vision of organization, balanced with the process and people components just discussed.

Challenge 2: Having a Plan

Many organizations do not have a robust plan outlining how their use of technology will evolve over time to better support the vision of their business. They seem to always be chasing the latest fire or the newest fad, never really progressing toward a well defined objective— they've lost their "azimuth." This results in a large amount of waste and disjointed information silos around the organization. Having a clearly defined information technology strategy is key to overcoming this problem. An overarching IT strategy for the organization should outline the vision of how IT will directly support meeting the business objectives of the organization. This strategy should define certain high-level initiatives that will be pursued in support of the business objectives. These high-level initiatives should then be decomposed into more specific deliverables that can be mapped to milestones. The IT strategy is different from the technology strategy that should support it, which I will discuss next. If the IT strategy is the "what" the technology strategy is the "how" of how the organization using technology as an enabler of the business.

Organizations must develop a robust technology strategy that will put in place the necessary tools to support the IT strategy. The technology strategy is normally created by the organization's CIO/CTO in conjunction with other executive leadership. As a leader, you should ensure that your CIO/CTO has defined a technology strategy that enables the organization to deliver highly agile, adaptive, integrated, and accelerated solutions that will meet the needs of people at all levels of the organization. The CIO/CTO should define a strategy that enables the effective creation of capability in support of the business and uses fewer resources in less time with greater success. This involves defining the methodology and governance as to how capability is delivered within the organization using defined toolsets, leveraging certain expertise, and so on. Again, this is the "how" of how an organization goes about delivering what has been defined in the IT strategy. The technology strategy should be robust in that it defines the repeatable mechanism by which IT solutions are routinely delivered. It should be sophisticated enough to manage the entire lifecycle of projects and to deliver varying requirements having similar qualities.

Challenge 3: Managing Expectations

Managing expectations is key to leaders and managers alike. As a leader we must set expectations through our example, communicating the vision and supporting the efforts of the CIO/CTO. A leader must be careful not to distract and must ensure that managers are empowered to move forward with their plans. Managers must ensure that they remain focused and do not create confusion by entertaining distractions, and they also must ensure that other managers are aware of the roadmap and have the opportunity to provide their feedback and ideas. When undertaking large efforts many, including myself, advocate working in a "stealth" mode. I personally find it better to operate this way, communicating high-level concepts to the masses but waiting until you have reached your ability to deliver solutions quickly before communicating the changes you intend to make throughout the organization. There is a fine line between communicating the vision, which is necessary so people are aware of where the business is going and feel prepared as that change comes, and setting immediate expectations in an environment where the ability to meet those expectations has not yet been established. People will look elsewhere quickly if they perceive an inability to meet their needs.

Challenge 4: Staying Focused, Keep Your Eye on the Prize

Staying focused on the vision is a must. If you can achieve a good IT strategy, have the right tools in place through your technology strategy, and you're effectively managing expectations, staying focused should be much easier. The key now is to focus on meeting the IT strategy without becoming distracted by what is commonly referred to as drive-bys. Drive -bys are when other managers and leaders will distract your staff with "quick" initiatives that they deem important at the time but distract from meeting the goals set forth in the IT strategy. While sometimes it is necessary to deliver quick wins to keep momentum and interest, it cannot be done at the risk of compromising the achievement of those goals. If you have a choice, focus on quick wins that contribute to the organization's higher level objectives. While they may be distracting from your plan, they still contribute toward the overall vision. In some cases, I have seen where segmenting staff into meeting these different requirements is effective. For instance, you can maintain a group of staff that is focused on meeting quick wins, while keeping a larger portion of your staff focused on meeting the longer term objectives of your initiative. This enables you to maintain the benefits that come with being able to deliver quick wins, but also ensures that you don't become so distracted that you can't meet the leadership objectives. Leaders help managers remain focused by ensuring that key milestones are set and progress can be demonstrated frequently and tangibly, meaning you can actually see new features or components at frequent intervals leading up to final delivery of capability. Using an iterative process to deliver solutions, similar to what is advocated by such agile development methodologies as SCRUM, is extremely useful in achieving this.

Q. Can you summarize the benefits of taking an LM type approach to your IT initiatives?

I've been thinking about the LM approach as I've been answering these questions and I can definitely see how the LM approach presented by Ed can be used as an effective guide to the technology initiatives within any organization. Many of the suggestions I made earlier for addressing challenges when implementing IT solutions map well to the LM model, and when I think about specific IT initiatives I've worked in the past I realize that many of the LM approaches applied in helping those projects to be successful.

Let's take, for example, an organization's Knowledge Management (KM) initiative. KM is a widely used term throughout many organizations today, having varying meanings to people. Ed presents the concept of a "knowledge based organization," one in which the organization recognizes the importance of information and uses this information in ways to become more efficient and effective in performing its daily mission. A KM program encompasses identifying the mechanisms through which that information is collected and implementing technology to capture it in a more structured manner so that it can be leveraged across the organization more efficiently and effectively. Ed mentions earlier that I worked with him at the White House Communications Agency (WHCA). WHCA is by far the most successful organization I have worked with in its ability to effectively capture information and leverage it elsewhere in the organization to achieve greater efficiency and effectiveness. They very much reflect the ideals that Ed presents in the LM. At the top of the organization, leadership established that WHCA would excel in its mission by leveraging technology to do more with fewer people, to do it effectively and efficiently, and to do it repeatedly in a systematic fashion. Leadership empowered the managers to take action and define a roadmap for implementing both a technology framework and processes for achieving continued innovation. Leadership communicated high-level goals that they believed would transform the organization and managers developed plans and executed them to deliver solutions to the workforce. Managers ensured a collaborative and iterative process that enabled participation and feedback from stakeholders so that change took hold and the fruits of innovation could be qualitatively and quantitatively measured across the organization. This continual interaction of people, process, and technology resulted in significant innovation across the command and, as I said, the most advanced KM organization I have seen or heard of during my career. Often other high-level agencies both foreign and domestic would come to WHCA for demonstrations; all were amazed by the level of capability that had been achieved and how quickly it had evolved from their previous visits.

The benefits of applying the LM are that you create a culture within your organization of trust based on empowerment, responsibility, and authority to achieve objectives as defined by leadership. It takes into account the three things that any business hinges on: its people (whether we mean employees, customers, or other stakeholders), the processes by which the organization functions (whether they are internal or customer-facing processes), and the technology used to enhance those processes. The LM represents a truly holistic approach to leading organizations to positive results.

Q. Based on your experience, what are the top three considerations or concerns you will address next time you implement a new technology into your organization?

First, I would maintain that it is critical to define your initiative in perspective with, and alignment with, the broader mission and vision of the organization. Everything that is planned should in some way map back to them. A good way to communicate this is through a project charter—outlining the scope, objectives, responsibilities, and outcomes expected for your initiative. Be sure to review this charter frequently and make it available to others.

Second, have a strategy. Your strategy should include incremental wins that when built up result in meeting the outcomes you defined in the charter and you can demonstrate to leaders for a periodic "azimuth check." For example, maybe I have an initiative to be able to ensure the organization has greater accuracy in its ability to target information to its staff of 50,000 people. My outcome might be to have accurate email distribution groups and portal audiences that will better enable me to target communications. Given the organization's personnel information is in disarray and user adoption of our company portal is limited, my intermediate goals could be such milestones as implement rules to ensure users are more likely to receive information by forcing their homepage to be our corporate portal. You can implement a process for people to validate their digital information periodically through the portal. Also, you could create several communities of interest groups based on information in the digital profiles and defined business rules to enable more granular targeting. These are all quick wins that could be demonstrated along the way and that collectively lead to the achievement of the targeted outcomes defined within the charter. The quick wins provide momentum along the way and are a logical progression to achieving the desire end state.

Finally, managing expectations is critical. Generally, I would say to under-promise and over-deliver. Most successful leaders and managers that I've worked with follow this general principle. Whether we are speaking with customers, leaders, or managers we need them to understand exactly what they are getting, not overselling or overpromising it, and how it will impact the organization. If in the end you can give them even more, that's gravy; just be sure what you promise is what you can deliver. It's better to be surprised by additional features than disappointed by ones that were promised but lacking in the final release. The more we can demonstrate what we are doing along the way to give them better awareness and input to the final solution, the greater the acceptance will be when the time comes to deliver those changes into the organization. Providing leaders with accurate expectations provides them greater opportunity to communicate those changes and for people to prepare themselves for those changes as they begin to be implemented with the organization.

Q. Finally, as you look back in your professional and personal life, share any final thoughts you have related to leadership/management and the impact it has had on your life.

My final thoughts for the audience of leaders reading this book are based on my experiences in the workplace and what I believe you can focus on to bring about the best from your people. I believe the most significant impact leaders can have on an organization is by focusing their efforts on eliciting positive behavior from their people to move toward the goals and objectives they've established. In my mind, this is the single most important thing a leader does. They do this by their example, their words, their encouragement, and their advocacy. Often we see this in storytelling, where leaders speak of innovation going on within their organization and valuing the positive behavior they seek to promote. Leaders are to inspire the talents of those on their team and to empower them so that the full potential of the organization can be recognized.

Critical to creating a thriving organization is getting the right people on the bus and the right people in the right seats, as Ed describes in a take away from the book *Good to Great*. All the credibility a leader brings can quickly be diminished by his/her inability to find the right leaders below them and to position people appropriately within the organization. A leader owes it to the people that work for him/her to get it right, because time is too valuable to expend it on people spinning their wheels in dysfunction.

Finally, loosen the reigns a bit. Give your people the opportunity to be innovative, be willing to accept a certain level of risk, and encourage people to be adventurous in their work— they'll be better for it and they themselves will be more accepting of the learning process of those around them. This makes the work place more exciting and results in the growing of future leaders in a world that could always use a few more good ones.

Ed's Final Thoughts

Pete and I have worked together closely on two KM initiatives, as well as other projects, and it is easy to see that we share similar views. Although I believe technology is the primary driver for change, I believe that successful implementation comes from individuals (leaders) who can spearhead change and solve problems based on their ability to appreciate the user's view and the technologist's view during design, development, and implementation of the technology. I believe much of Pete's success comes because of his talent to understand these two perspectives. I have noticed younger, more junior leaders possess this same talent. Are you able to do this? Much of the reason I see this in more junior leaders is that formal education has evolved to develop a hybrid of technology and operational or business functional degrees. This is absolutely the right direction. You really need to have both skill sets to be successful when it comes to implementing technology.

Chapter 6

Strategic Planning – Yes, You Need It!

*If you know the enemy and know yourself, you need not fear the results
of a hundred battles. If you know yourself but not the
enemy, for every victory gained you will also suffer a defeat. If you know
neither the enemy nor yourself, you will succumb in every battle.*
- Sun Tzu

Strategic planning is an area that is too often neglected in lieu of fighting daily battles. Unfortunately, this is the work that is most important for your organization to have sustained success. The ability to step out of the day-to-day fray and look at long-term changes that can improve problem areas or create future opportunities is a skill that not many people seem to have. Strategic planning is appropriate for leaders at all levels, not just senior leaders. The quickest way for an individual or a team to start realizing its full potential is to spend more time doing quality strategic planning and less time fighting fires.

In this chapter we will look at the importance of having a vision for the future and a mission statement that states your purpose and how it supports your vision. We also will look at how an operational focus helps you keep a nested approach in which each individual's role and goals support the organization's mission and vision. We will end this chapter looking at the art of strategic thinking, which seems to be lost on many of today's leaders but is vital to moving any organization forward.

Operational Alignment with Mission and Vision

Vision without action is merely a dream. Action without vision just passes the time. Vision with action can change the world.
- Joel A. Barker

The LM provides a foundation that can help you and your team align roles and goals with the bigger picture of the organization's mission and vision for the future. Similarly, the overall awareness for your purpose within your COIs provides the synergy discussed earlier in which passionate and empowered people can make positive things happen within an organization and across organizational boundaries.

As you begin to look at the LM concept in a more holistic manner it will become more apparent why it is important for individuals within a team to take an active role in developing organizational goals and mission and vision statements, as well as identifying their roles and goals in each. Each of these areas should be in harmony with the others. The positive effects of such an approach include personal development and individual buy-in to the team's mission or purpose. The benefits to the organization include multiple perspectives and an empowered workforce. The LM provides an empowering approach to doing business that continually looks at how an organization can work better tomorrow than it does today. There is no way for an individual or organization to perform to their full potential if they do not understand their role in relation to the bigger picture.

Throughout my professional career I have continually grown to fully appreciate the value of how important it is to have a team of individuals that takes an active role in developing and/or refining the mission and vision of the team. An approach that documents the organization's mission, vision, and goals, as well as the individual's roles and goals, can be extremely productive when done correctly. I have seen strategic planning packaged a half dozen different ways with different titles and meanings for such words as "goals" and "objectives." I will provide some concepts and views that I hope will stimulate your thoughts about how you and your organization want to package your approach. Don't fall into the trap of arguing about semantics; think beyond that and focus on the spirit of the approach.

As an Army officer I was exposed to a nesting process that produced a Mission Essential Task List (METL). If done properly, the METL supported your mission statement as well as your higher headquarters' mission. The production of the METL would capture individual tasks, collective tasks (team tasks), and leader tasks. The METL was an all-encompassing document that would help you focus your energy and resources appropriately. Based on your inability to perform a task to standard you may spend more time or money in training or equipping your team in that specific function. In addition to this method, I have worked within and been exposed to similar methods that organizations use to maintain their focus. These different approaches have many similarities but use different terminology. Although the terminology is different the overall intent is to align individual and team tasks so they support the overall organizational mission and goals.

Like many things in life, strategic planning is productive if you go about it in a constructive manner, recognizing the benefits that can be gained. I have seen and participated in many drills that have been a terrible waste of time. The reason for failure may vary in detail but it generally comes down to people either being unaware of what to do, unable to do it, or unwilling to do it. Hopefully, it is not the last reason or you have a real problem to solve. A successful approach to strategic planning is to instill it in your daily activities with periodic, focused efforts that bring it to the forefront for everyone. Such an approach incorporates recurring team meetings, the azimuth check assessment, and individual performance counseling.

For example, a newly formed organization should spend a focused effort up front, establishing its mission and vision statements. Roles and goals need to be established early on so that people have a sense of purpose and organizational standards. A method that incorporates individuals at all levels will produce a solid strategic plan. Using the LM as a guide, the plan can address the people, processes, and technologies that are the foundation of the first principle of the LM: people, process, and technology map to every organizational function. Thinking from this framework will facilitate accurate and thorough documentation to support mission, vision, and goals.

As your organization matures, don't make the tragic mistake of thinking that strategic planning does not need as much focus as it did earlier. If you work within the LM you understand that continual change is inevitable and you will either create the change proactively or be forced to react to change. The proactive approach enables you to keep a well-communicated and strategically aligned approach that affects everything from the organizational vision to individual roles and goals. A proactive approach to strategic planning is appropriate for all members of the organization. The amount of time spent in looking out to the future is proportionate to your position. More senior leaders should spend almost all their time looking strategically at the future. More junior leaders should spend less time looking at the future direction of the organization and most of their energy accomplishing the established goals. If good work was done upfront to align individuals' goals with the organization's goals then there is a natural connection in developing and working towards all the goals. The recurring azimuth check is a great way to keep leaders at all levels appropriately focused on the strategic aspects of the organization.

Although senior leaders spend more time looking at the big picture, I still encourage the junior leaders to find time to look at the big picture. The time will be well spent for their professional development and for the organization's long-term benefit. You cannot be as valuable in principles 2 and 3 if you don't spend time looking at the bigger picture. Senior leaders can encourage this exploration by discussing this informally or during performance evaluations. In addition to the recurring azimuth assessment, regularly scheduled sessions that talk about the state of the organization (similar to the Presidential State of the Union) can provide an opportunity to stimulate strategic thought at all levels of the organization. These different techniques all contribute to creating a knowledge-based organization that is operationally focused and ready for the ever-changing future.

There are great advantages to having each subordinate team within your organization function within the same framework (such as the LM) as the parent organization. This awareness promotes an organizational atmosphere that is conducive to producing results and continually looking for ways to get better at your mission. Many of the key characteristics for people that we discussed in Chapter 3 are developed and refined based on this understanding and the atmosphere created. The most important as-

pect is the development of future leaders. There is nothing more important to an organization than continually developing future leaders. Future
leaders are developed when they are exposed to strategic planning, which
enhances their understanding of the big picture. Too often, senior leaders
feel that strategic planning and brainstorming is only appropriate for the
senior leaders and they miss opportunities to get other perspectives from
more junior leaders.

I once worked for a General Officer who was extremely removed
from his organization. His demeanor and leadership style inhibited junior
leader development. Looking in hindsight, I believe he was insecure with
his abilities and tried to make up for this by always showing us that he
was the boss. He frequently reminded us of that by pointing to the star on
his shoulder and referring to his position and status. Once, when a co-
worker (we will call him Jim) was briefing the General on how he intended to perform a certain task, the General told Jim that he wanted the
task performed in a different manner. When Jim pointed out, in a respectful manner, that the regulation required it to be done the way he had mentioned, the General told him that the regulation was wrong and that he
must have a misprint of the regulation. This is one example of many in
which the General went to extremes to be "right." Unfortunately, we all
have probably seen leaders who rely on rank, position, or status to lead.
These leaders are usually marginally effective at best and often any positive results are generally short lived or accomplished because of strong
informal leaders within the organization.

Aside from being belligerent and rude with the people that worked
for him, this General had real issues when someone disagreed with him in
either what needed to be done or how to do it. You can imagine how the
entire staff was stifled and turned into "yes men." The environment that
was created was one where nothing got done unless the General said to
do it. Because
his compe-
tence was
questionable
at best, there
was not much

> There is nothing more important to an organization than
> continually developing future leaders. Future leaders are
> developed when they are exposed to strategic planning
> which enhances their understanding of the big picture.

true production coming from our staff section.

While I worked for this General I witnessed first-hand during my
performance evaluation how he viewed the junior officers that worked
for him and his lack of appreciation for the importance of letting us think
about the big picture. During the period of performance, I had done a
very good job bringing to fruition an aggressive new technology proposal
that won the command more than $40 million in grant money. It was now

time for my performance evaluation and the General gave me an adequate evaluation but not the glowing evaluation that I had thought I had earned. When I saw the evaluation, I confronted the General and asked why I did not get a top evaluation block and referred to all the things that were accomplished with a program that I started from scratch. His reply was something that you may expect from a Dilbert cartoon. He stated that although I did very well, I must understand that sometimes I am "too visionary." He went on to explain that I think too strategically and that I was not paid to think. He, as a General, is paid to think and I am paid to do what I am told. He elaborated on these points and then asked me if anyone had ever told me that before. I was dumbfounded and I told the General that, yes, I did have bosses that said that I had the ability to think more strategically and grasp the bigger picture. I went on to say that every other time my bosses recognized this as a positive trait and that he was the only one to ever say this was a negative trait. Just for the record, Army leadership doctrine emphasizes the importance of leaders at all levels understanding the bigger picture. I still shake my head at the exchange that took place in his office. This was a General Officer in the Army who in less than 10 minutes communicated a leadership perspective that was not only completely out of line with the Army philosophy, but left me wondering how in the world a person like that made it to the General Officer level.

That story describes an environment that discourages initiative and ultimately limits the organization to adapt to change because of the lack of strategic vision within the organization. The LM, like any organizational framework, is only as good as the individuals who execute within that structure. The use of the LM to make your organization better is as dependent on people, processes, and technology as any other functional area within the organization. As we will discuss, the LM does provide an effective method to help stimulate thought and action by maintaining a productive operational perspective with respect to people, processes, and technology development.

An Operational Mindset — Mission-Focused and Change-Oriented

You are today where your thoughts have brought you; you will be tomorrow where your thoughts take you. - James Allen

An operational mindset is one that is focused on successful execution of the mission, as well as continual improvement. The LM embraces this mindset. The LM recognizes the importance of monitoring and measuring the results produced by people, process, and technology today. At the same time, the LM provides the stimulus for making changes in support of continual improvement.

Change is inevitable. Individuals and organizations not only should recognize this but should embrace change. However, too many people are scared of change. It is this fear of change and the unwillingness to accept the thought that change is constant that is the problem. Implementing change can be a challenge, but like most organizational activities it comes down to executing a good plan that addresses the people, processes, and technology aspects of the change. Employing a method to change that enables everyone to participate is not easy but it is essential to the success of implementing the change at hand. Too many change initiatives are supported half-heartedly in both planning and execution, giving the appearance that the idea to change was wrong when, in reality, the weak implementation of the change initiative is what was wrong. John Kotter's book, *Leading Change*, does a superb job of capturing the challenges organizations face when implementing changes and how to overcome these challenges. Like other identified best practices, the LM captures the spirit of much of Kotter's principles.

As you look at your role within the organization you need to recognize your responsibilities for identifying change opportunities and in executing those changes. Recognizing that everyone plays a role in change is a powerful way to make sure that your organization is continually optimizing its performance and is not reacting to change but creating change. When I was a Lieutenant one of my positions was as the battalion logistics officer. My job was to oversee all the internal logistics support for an 800-soldier support battalion. My responsibilities were in broad areas relative to logistical and material readiness, real property management and utilization,

> **Too many change initiatives are supported half heartedly in both planning and execution giving the appearance that the idea to change was wrong when in reality the weak implementation of the change initiative is what was wrong.**

financial management, food service operations, property accountability, and battalion transportation and maintenance activities. This was a wide range of responsibilities. This also was when desktop computers were just starting to make an impact in offices and businesses. While I was in this position, our battalion was issued 10 standalone desktop computers. We provided one to each company and each staff section. Within one year, we had completely changed how we performed the majority of our functions to communicate and monitor our logistics responsibilities within the battalion. We automated processes that were performed with calculators, grease pencils, and typewriters, creating efficiencies that impacted the entire battalion. As time went on, we had two more computers and automated more aspects of our mission. Over the course of a year we, as a team, started to function differently and solve problems in a different manner. Everyone on the team was actively looking at how to do things better based on having a few standalone computers available to us.

As a young Lieutenant, I was not savvy enough to recognize that I should identify roles and goals for my team that supported the concept of continual improvement. Although they implemented some improvements on their own, it would have been more beneficial to them and my section as a whole to formally challenge them to seek continual improvement. The LM captures the intent of continual improvement with the second and third principles:

- Principle 2 — Continual navigation involving people, process, and technology leads to improvement.
- Principle 3 — A direction change in people, process, or technology requires an azimuth check of the other two.

If we fast-forward more than 20 years, where in almost all my business or COI interactions I, at a minimum, mentally gain an understanding of the group mission and how daily operations are supported by the individual roles within a people, processes, and technology framework. I am quick to gain an understanding of what goals are identified to facilitate future improvements. It is an awareness that was not present early in my professional career.

The desktop computer example demonstrates how a small change can have a large impact. This change occurred two decades before I had captured the LM as a concept; however, it fits right in line with principles 2 and 3. With a technology change we adjusted people and processes to take advantage of the new technology. Not being aware of the interdependency of people, process, and technology, we stumbled through these changes and did not get as much from the change initiative as we could have. Now, being more aware of how people, processes, and technology interrelate with each other, I am able to work within the COI to get the most out of the change initiative.

If you take the time to review the change initiatives that you have experienced, I think you will find that no matter how unique the circumstances, the principles of the LM in relation to people, processes, and technology are constant. The LM provides a framework that allows you to maintain an awareness of people, processes, and technology and manage the roles and goals in making the changes to enhance your mission performance. This awareness and an operational mindset enable you to review any situation in your organization to find and fix shortfalls or to look for opportunities for improvements. An operational mindset keeps you focused on analyzing your performance for efficiency and effectiveness. Although we will talk about relationships in a later chapter, it is important to recognize that it is through relationships that you are able to meet your responsibilities within your role.

The LM Influence — Roles and Relationships

Stay committed to your decisions but stay flexible in your approach.
- Tom Robbins

Roles are used to identify who will perform what tasks and goals to what standard. Identifying roles is essential to be able to measure and monitor individual and team performance. I believe to successfully identify roles one needs to keep an operational mindset. An operational mindset recognizes that every aspect of an organization is connected operationally—actions in one functional area impact other areas. One leader's operational mission is another's administrative or support function. I spent my entire military career focused on supporting "operational units" with either logistics support or with communications support. As a leader, these functions were my operational functions. The key point is that all functions within an organization are linked to the organizational mission. When a function is mapped to the mission, it is easier to identify the importance of all aspects of the organization and how important the

> **An operational mindset recognizes that every aspect of an organization is connected operationally - actions in one functional area impact other areas.**

function is to mission success.

Many organizations identify the roles of individuals. However, often these are only done to meet the organization's HR requirements. Only a small number of organizations go beyond the roles and identify goals to support those roles. This is really what leaders/managers should be doing, but unfortunately they are caught up too often with small issues that have little to no strategic impact on the organization. By keeping an operational mindset it is much easier to identify roles and goals that will truly enhance the mission of the organization.

Have you ever been a part of a team or an organization where you didn't know your role, your goals, and how your role and goals supported the bigger organization? Remember the simple soccer example from Chapter1? Imagine, if you will, a business where people show up daily and wait to be told what to do. Lower-level managers wait for an email before they perform any action. I bet many of you are laughing now because you have been in such an organization. Do you want to continue to drift through life waiting for an email to tell you what to do and when to do it? If your answer is yes, well then, this book and the concepts of the LM are not for you. If your answer is you want to take charge of your life— your organization— then now is the time to do something.

Pretend for a moment that you are a mid-level manager in a semi-large (just fewer than 800 people) company (Government contractor). You manage a subsection of a program that provides IT support services on site for your Government client. You have been there for six months but your company has had the contract for several years. Now that you have been there for six months you follow up with your team (12 people total) to individually talk to them about their responsibilities. Using questions from the LM Azimuth Check, as well as other questions you developed specific to the program, you quickly find out that many of your people have no idea about the overall purpose behind the tasks they perform. You further find out that almost half the tasks they are performing on the surface don't appear to be related to the statement of work (SOW) within your contract. What now you ask?

The LM should be used as a guide as you set up or adjust your organizational structure. As your organization changes with the times so should your organizational structure. After all, your organizational structure is based on your mission and the roles of the individuals within the organization. Using the azimuth check approach that we have discussed throughout this book, if a task or a series of tasks becomes obsolete because of technology, it may be appropriate to change the organization and even eliminate positions or create new ones. We will talk about relationships in a later chapter but recognize that people hold positions, and a position may appear to be more or less relevant based on the person holding the position. Don't be scared to change the organization to maximize your team's strengths and mitigate the weaknesses. *Figure 2* provides a more traditional organizational view of the LM, a hierarchal view that you would normally associate with an organization.

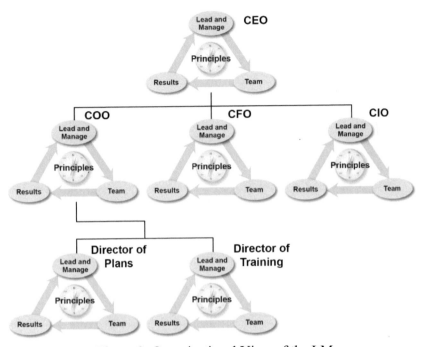

Figure 2: Organizational View of the LM

A more holistic view of the LM is depicted in **_Figure 3_** as a frame-work for each individual's interactions within their COIs. This is a broader view of how the LM can provide an efficient and effective approach to all your relationships based on a COI perspective. This method recognizes that you have different roles based on the interactions you have with the many different groups of people with whom you have a relationship. The LM provides an effective approach for you to develop those relationships in the best interest of the common good for all involved. Whether it is your formal role in your job, a role in a work related committee, or a church or civic role, the LM can be used accordingly to increase your awareness of your roles in each.

Figure 3: COI View of the LM

Understanding your roles and the relationship you have with the other people involved in your COIs will help you be more productive. Organizations can grow exponentially when leaders at all levels gain a better appreciation for their roles and how they apply to the mission and vision of the organization. The LM facilitates this understanding and will also stimulate your ability to think more strategically.

Strategic Thinking — You Must Find the Time

A man who does not think for himself does not think at all. - Oscar Wilde

Strategic planning is a weakness in many organizations. As we have identified, often the problem is a lack of understanding with regard to the mission and vision of the organization and how individuals' roles and goals support the organization's purpose. This lack of understanding has much to do with how little an emphasis is put on "strategic thinking." Long-term success is dependent on the ability to optimize performance today and be prepared for changes in the future. Continual improvement and preparedness comes from always looking at how to do things better (principle 2). Unfortunately, too often the strategically significant events we have planned fall prey to the short-term firefights that we face day in and day out.

There are many time-management techniques designed to help individuals increase their awareness of how they spend their time during the day. The intent of these techniques is to help people increase production by identifying where time is wasted. Often, time is spent working on less important issues or actions in lieu of more important ones. Individuals mistakenly think that the daily fires that they are normally consumed with are more important than the strategic tasks that may not have a short suspense. I do not intend to talk specifically about time-management techniques in this book but I do recommend that you set aside time specific to longer-term, more strategic tasks at least on a weekly basis. If you are a senior leader you really should set aside a large amount of time daily. As a senior leader this should be your primary role and you should have recurring meetings and work sessions related to the various organizational functions in the content of the current operational picture and the movement towards improvement.

It is important not only to increase the time and energy spent thinking strategically, but equally important to monitor how conducive your time is to quality thinking. Because we tend to live such busy lives, spending quality time thinking seems hard to do. What is conducive to quality thinking time varies for every individual. There are a few things that are common to all. First, you must mentally be ready to focus on the subject at hand. Also, put yourself in an environment that supports uninterrupted thinking. Finally, take the time to think about the subject from many different perspectives.

The environment that supports my best strategic thinking may surprise you. For the last 15 years or more, I found that I can do my best thinking when I am exercising. A morning workout and run provide me about an hour a day to think. This is my individual time that is rarely interrupted and provides a great opportunity to focus my thoughts on a specific

> Often individuals mistakenly think that the daily fires that they are normally consumed with are more important than the strategic tasks that may not have a short suspense.

subject. I routinely use this time for my most strategic thinking. I often think about the tougher problems that one of my clients may be struggling with during these morning sessions. I have thought through many of the concepts provided in this book during my exercise time. Running may not be for you, but figure out what activity or setting is best to do your strategic thinking. Maybe it is during your commute to and from work? As you settle into your routine to support strategic thinking, remember to get outside your normal mindset and stimulate new ways of looking at the issues from alternate perspectives.

A thorough understanding of issues or initiatives, as well as creative problem solving, is enhanced by your ability to consider different perspectives. It is natural to fall back on our experience and individual perspective and come to a conclusion of what needs to be done. However, this approach limits innovation and progress. Depending on the perspectives of others within the COI, it may curb buy-in to the decision and ultimately undermine the initiative. The ability to view issues from many perspectives is a powerful talent that will help you in your leadership role of communicating and guiding your team.

Of course one way to consider other perspectives is to actively solicit other opinions. Get the opinions of different team members at all levels. I also recommend getting other stakeholder opinions within the COI. Finally, it never hurts to have a solid outside perspective. My experience as a consultant has been that an independent opinion is valuable to leaders at all levels. Don't expect drastic 180-degree differences in how you view a subject and how a consultant views it. I most often find my views are similar to the client's view with slight differences. What you really get from an independent consultant is a few key nuggets of information that are normally overlooked by people who are too close to the issue to see the alternative perspective. One of those alternative perspectives should be your competition's perspective. Don't underestimate your competition and how they will react to the factors that you are studying. The value of using all these different methods to gather information also provides you with opportunities to create and foster strong relationships with people inside and outside your organization. The value of these relationships will become more apparent in the next chapter when we specifically talk about relationships.

Conclusion

As you continue to think about how you and your organization as a whole deal with the strategic challenges you face, consider how the LM facilitates strategic thinking. The holistic aspects of people, processes, and technology are at the forefront for consideration. Alignment of the mission and vision with roles and goals provides a solid foundation of purpose for everyone on the team. Additionally, the cyclic approach of communicating a message, developing a plan, and monitoring and measuring the execution of the plan will lead to feedback. This feedback fosters adjustments that keep you continually engaged in improving performance. As you balance communicating with all stakeholders about what needs to be done with thinking about how to improve upon your performance, you look at opportunities to get their perspective on the challenges that the organization faces. Using these perspectives and outside opinions to help you look at things from all angles you are prepared to make decisions, monitor those decisions, and appropriately adjust the decisions. The LM keeps you focused on the strategically valuable issues and limits the amount of time that you spend on minor issues that arise throughout the day.

The following table captures benefits related to leadership/ management and to the organization as a whole when you take an approach to strategic thinking that considers the key concepts discussed in this chapter.

Key concepts and benefits to you as a leader and to the organization

Operational alignment with mission and vision – aligning roles and goals

Benefits to the Leader/Manager:	Benefits to the Organization:
• Your tool to grow individuals and teams is centered around this alignment	• Creates a knowledgeable team with a focused effort to achieve success

An operational mindset – mission focused and change oriented

Benefits to the Leader/Manager:	Benefits to the Organization:
• Continually judge the expenditure of resources against your mission success • Ask yourself and your team what can be done to improve the current approach	• Maximum use of people and resources • Encourages creative thinking that can lead to improvements

The LM influence – roles and relationships

Benefits to the Leader/Manager:	Benefits to the Organization:
• Recognize that roles are influenced by people and organize accordingly	• Maximizes individual strengths to create synergy for success

Strategic thinking – the difference between success and excellence

Benefits to the Leader/Manager:	Benefits to the Organization:
• Facilitates your understanding of COIs and the many perspectives within each	• Creates well-rounded individuals who can grow into the organization's senior leaders.

While providing KM consulting services to the Navy command, I met and worked with Jeff Pottinger, Senior Director, Cowan and Associates (C&A). C&A provides strategy, supply chain management, program management, IT advisory support, performance management, change management, and business process improvement services to help clients achieve superior results in the public and executive education sectors. C&A was ranked 304th on the 2009 *Inc.* 500 list of fastest growing private companies in America. While I was working on the KM effort with the Navy command, Jeff was providing consulting services focused on strategic planning and organizational change. I was immediately impressed by Jeff's depth of knowledge on the subject and his ability to communicate sometimes very advanced concepts in simple and easy-to-understand terms. Jeff's ability to motivate and lead teams stems from a career that includes 30 years of progressive leadership and management experience in DoD, big-box retail, and consulting. I have seen Jeff bring together various best practices and techniques based on his expertise in supply chain management, retail operations, program management, executive education, and business development to streamline and improve operations. I asked Jeff to provide his thoughts on strategic planning and how the concepts within this chapter are relevant to any organization or individual because I know he will provide the simple, sound advice that will resonate well with leaders reading this book.

Strategic Thinking and Planning — More than a Check in the Box

Q. How do you ensure strategic planning can be productive at all levels within an organization?

Throughout my career in the Navy, Circuit City, or in my consulting work, I have been continually amazed at the lack of real strategic thinking and planning. Most organizations I have worked with, particularly Government organizations, treat strategic planning as just another task. It's something everyone else does, so I better do it too. All too often, it becomes a drill to "update" the old strategic plan, add some great pictures of our products and people, create a nice slogan, throw in a glossy cover, print it, distribute it, and then watch it disappear into file cabinets or onto a bookshelf to collect dust. There is no real environmental scanning... no real thinking about the future... no real scenario planning... no real development of high-level objectives... no ownership assigned for these objectives... no creation of team and individual tasks to push these objectives forward... and, generally, only the involvement of a few select individuals. And, most disappointing, I find little or no accountability for achieving the objectives or the tasks. The focus of many organizations' strategic planning efforts is not on how to drive future growth, or how to build market share, or how to prepare for the latest competitor within your space, or how to align the company. Rather, the focus is on just getting the task done so it can be checked off the task list and they can move on to the next task or crisis. Without real strategic thinking and planning, organizations are doomed to mediocrity (Government), or doomed to failure (Circuit City).

I don't intend to use this section to outline a strategic planning model and ask the reader to use it. There are plenty of strategic planning models out there, any one of which could be used to help move your organization forward. Just Google "strategic planning" and you will have a plethora of alternatives from which to choose. Ed offers his insights and ideas in this chapter and throughout the book. Rather, my challenge to each reader is to ask yourself whether you are really committed to adding strategic planning to your leadership toolbox. If you are, great, you can skip the rest of this chapter. But, if you aren't, ask yourself why.

Q. Elaborate on how leaders can use strategic planning as a tool for success.

My fundamental guiding principle/leadership philosophy is: Anything is possible... and, I don't believe in the word "can't." In almost every case, when I hear someone say they can't do something, it is either because they don't know how or because they choose not to. If they don't know how, it is the leader's responsibility to teach them or find them the training so they will know how. If they choose not to, it is the leader's responsibility to find out why. If they are choosing not to because of a valid business impediment, then it is up to the leader to help them remove that obstacle. If they are choosing not to just because they don't want to and have no valid business reason to not do it, then it's up to the leader to help them find another job.

It is POSSIBLE for each of you to incorporate strategic planning/ thinking into your toolbox. Whether you lead an organization, a department, a team, or are just an individual worker, you CAN choose to incorporate strategic planning/thinking into your toolbox. I have found that the best way to push a new idea forward is to give it a try yourself and let the results convince your boss that it's the right thing to do. If you've never done any strategic planning/thinking before, do the Google search, read some articles or a book, and give it a shot. A couple of books I've used include Michael Porter's *Competitive Strategy* and Kaplan's and Norton's books on the balanced scorecard. The more you practice it and read how others do it, the better you will become. If you are just an individual working your own projects, conduct your strategic planning/thinking on your own and incorporate it into how you approach your individual project work. If you work in a team, suggest strategic planning/thinking during your next team meeting and offer to take the lead in holding a planning session. If you lead a team or department, ask your team if any of them have experience with strategic planning/thinking. For those who don't, offer up some training. For those who do, ask them to take the lead in setting up and running a session. You get the picture. This stuff isn't rocket science— it just takes someone to get it started, a little training, and a commitment to give it a shot. I think you will be surprised at the impact it has on your ability to do the right things and do them well.

Alignment — The Key to Linking Strategy to Execution

Q. How do you transform planning into execution and results?

I like using the term "alignment" as a link between strategy and execution. When my car is out of alignment, the wheels are attempting to head off in every direction, the ride is bumpy, and it is very difficult to get where I'm going. And I'm not too happy with the experience. The same is true for an organization. You can have a great strategy, but if time isn't taken to align the strategy with the people, processes, and technology of the organization, you can fully expect a bumpy ride— possibly in the wrong direction— and you will probably have a few disgruntled employees along the way.

What exactly is meant by the term "alignment"? George Labovitz and Victor Rosansky, in their book, *The Power of Alignment*, describe alignment as a set of actions that:

- "Connect their employees' behavior to the mission of the company, turning intentions into actions.
- Link teams and processes to the changing needs of customers.
- Shape business strategy with real-time information from customers.
- Create a culture in which these elements all work together seamlessly."

To be effective, each department, team, and individual must be aligned toward the same objectives, or like our cars, we'll find a bumpy road along the way. Higher-level objectives, down to individual actions, must support the strategy to be effective.

The simplest method I've seen used is to cascade the organization's strategic objectives down through each level of the organization all the way down to the individual. Identify specific actions that an organization/team/individual must take to achieve the objective, determine how you will measure success, identify who is responsible for the action, and reward them/hold them accountable for their performance. I used this method with great success while serving as the Supply Officer aboard a United States Navy helicopter carrier. One of the key objectives of the ship was to maintain its warfighting capabilities at the highest state of readiness. As the supply/logistics department supporting the ship, one of our roles was to provide repair parts to maintain shipboard equipment. I met with my direct reports responsible for repair parts inventory to discuss what key actions we needed to take to support the ship's readiness. We agreed (after discussion with our customers and some negotiations amongst ourselves) that we could best support the ship by minimizing the time from when a repair part was requested to the time we provided it to the customer. That became the key measure of how we would evaluate our performance for supporting equipment readiness and my direct report became responsible for the performance measurement and actions required to improve it. After further discussions with division personnel, they agreed that the key actions needed to be taken included improving our onboard repair part stock, and minimizing the shipping time when repair parts were not available aboard the ship. The division officer and his personnel determined who was responsible for those actions and gave them ownership for improving their specific performance measurements. We created a process for capturing the data and we met twice monthly to review the department goal. If necessary, we drilled down into the division goals and all the way down to the individual goals. We discussed actions taken to improve performance, met with our customers, anticipated problems over the next two weeks, and specific actions to minimize their impact. Fully aligned with what we needed to do, we quickly improved parts availability and delivery and significantly improved the ship's warfighting capability.

From my personal perspective, aligning my organization was all about communication and teamwork. It wasn't rocket science. You can start building an effective tool box by taking the techniques Ed outlined throughout this book and adapting them to fit you. The key, once again, is being personally committed to taking the steps necessary to gain alignment. Determine the organization's key objectives. With your team, identify what you need to do to help the organization achieve their objectives. Figure out who is responsible within your organization and how you will measure their success. Help them determine the key actions necessary to meet the objective. Do this with each COI within your organization and you will take a giant step toward alignment, and successful execution.

Innovation and Change — A Difficult, Ongoing Process

Q. How does strategic planning promote innovation and change?

What I have found, particularly in my work with Government, is that innovation and change are hard. The culture of most organizations doesn't accept change and fears innovation. Whether it's fear of losing a job, fear of doing something new and uncomfortable, or just plain complacency, I haven't found too many Government organizations that truly embrace innovation and change as a part of their corporate culture. Eventually, it boils down to individuals so budget-oriented that they fear "new" projects will pull funding from their programs and they either vehemently defend their programs, or actively fight the innovation/change. Even when the facts and numbers support the change, you can almost hear this common refrain: "We've tried that before and it didn't work" or "we've always done it this way and we've been successful." As a result, the organization doesn't change to face new conditions, or if it does change, it changes very slowly. The result: mediocrity.

I have always felt that innovation and change were inexorably linked with strategic planning and strategic thinking. As any organization, large or small, begins to anticipate the future and align their organization to meet it, they inevitably change something... products, markets, technology, processes. It is difficult to maintain long-term success without change/innovation. As the old saying goes, you can't continue to do the same thing over and over again and expect different results. A dynamic strategic planning/thinking process will stimulate an ongoing drive toward innovation and change within your organization.

The key to driving a change in corporate culture to accept innovation and change is to involve the entire workforce in the development of the strategic plan and the cascading of the resultant action plans. Leaders throughout the organization must communicate the corporate mission and vision in clear terms, then involve everyone in their team/COI in the process of developing the objectives and actions necessary to achieve the mission and vision. This creates ownership of the plan and a clear understanding of roles and responsibilities. As a result, there is a greater willingness to accept the innovations and changes they helped develop.

Strategic communication is more than just outward. It is inward as well and is a key responsibility of leaders, regardless of their relative position within the organization. Even if your organization doesn't have a formal strategic planning process, there is no reason you can't implement one within your COI. The benefits gained from involving your team in the process of defining the way ahead for them are immeasurable. And, it's the right thing to do.

Anything is Possible —
Thoughts on Leadership and Management

Q. Finally, as you look back in your professional and personal life, share any final thoughts you have related to leadership/management and the impact it has had on your life.

I strongly concur with Ed's thoughts that leadership and management, are intertwined and all of us, no matter what level of the organization, require skills in both. Early in our careers, we generally have more management traits and fewer leadership traits. As we progress in our careers, we take on larger leadership roles that require fewer management responsibilities. However, I've found that many organizations don't have a formal process for training their emerging leaders to give them the necessary skills to lead. The organization promotes based on proven management/technical skills and expects the leader to inherit the leadership skills necessary for their new role. If your organization doesn't have formal leadership training, take the initiative and find your own training. Whether it's pursuing an advanced degree, taking an executive education course, picking up a book on leadership, or finding a mentor who demonstrates the leadership traits you admire, take responsibility for your own training. I have found throughout my career that the most successful leaders are lifelong learners and they take responsibility for their own training.

I'd be remiss if I didn't circle back to my underlying philosophy. Remember, anything is possible and "can't" isn't in my vocabulary. You either don't know how or you are choosing not to do something. Whenever you are faced with a situation where you feel something can't be done... ask yourself why. If you don't know how, take responsibility for getting yourself trained. If there is a business impediment that is keeping you from moving forward, find a way to remove the obstacle... with your team, your boss, and your peers. If you find yourself saying that you know how to do something and there is no business impediment, you just don't want to do it... you might be part of the problem.

Ed's Final Thoughts

Jeff's insight reinforces the importance of thinking strategically as a way of life. This is a trait that will serve you well. Taking the time to figure out where you want to be in a year, five years, 10 years, and so on makes the difference in achieving the success you desire. Most people have no direction in life and don't require a leadership map because they don't know where they are now and where they want to go. As a leader you must first understand the importance of focusing your energy toward obtaining your goals. Once you understand this and live this at the individual level you can then apply this to your organization or team. You will be most successful in strategic planning if you lead by example with your own life. First take charge of your life; becoming a visionary leader will follow naturally.

Chapter 7

Relationships –
The Key Ingredient to Enabling Success

All relationships of people to each other rest, as a matter of course, upon the precondition that they know something about each other.
- Georg Simmel

Building relationships with the people within your COIs should be a high priority. Ultimately it is your relationship with others that stimulates action and hopefully progress. As a leader, your challenge is to understand and appreciate all the people with whom you work— up, down, and across organizational lines. The only way you can do this is to take the time to build a solid relationship. As we discussed in Chapter 3, the foundation of a solid relationship is built on trust. Trust is developed based on your interactions with each individual. You will be judged daily on how you interact with people and these interactions form the foundation of the relationships that you will build.

Once a strong relationship is developed, you can pick up the phone anytime and talk to that person. It is this type of relationship that you should strive for with the people who are the most important in your life. Obviously, family and personal friends fit into this category. Your intent should be to add other professional relationships to this category. I would suggest starting with the people with whom you work most closely. I would further suggest that your goal be that you give your best to create a positive relationship with everyone with whom you interact. That does not mean that you need to develop the same relationship with each person; it means that you should be able to create an appropriate relationship that is genuine and constructive.

Is your relationship strong enough to ask the advice of your team members and get their honest opinion?

The wisest and most successful leaders understand the importance of maintaining strong relationships with the people with whom they interact daily. The best leaders acknowledge that relationships affect all functional areas within an organization. For this reason, the more energy and resources spent on relationship management the more productive the work environment will become. In today's highly competitive market for talent, a leader must be able to create and foster strong relationships. A one-size-fits-all mentality does not go far. Like any other aspect of a business, relationship management can be made easier when you increase your knowledge and awareness of the subject, as well as understand your particular environment. The LM provides an easy way for you to look at the people, processes, and technology available to enhance your ability to create and manage productive relationships.

Relationship Management and the LM

I do not believe in things: I believe in relationships.—Georges Braque

Throughout this book we have talked about relationships. Because relationships impact every aspect of your organization (and your life for that matter) it makes sense that this subject comes up repeatedly. This also is why it is appropriate for us to bring in the LM and look at how this frame-

> **Using the LM as a guide for how you interact within your organizational and COI relationships will help you focus your attention when and where it is needed based on your role (s) and the mission at hand.**

work can help you manage your relationships.

Using the LM as a guide for how you interact within your organizational and COI relationships will help you focus your attention when and where it is needed based on your role and the mission at hand. This framework provides a proactive approach for an individual to interact with other team members using leader and manager skills appropriately to build a strong and productive relationship. The LM is an appropriate framework for every individual to use as a guide in all their COI interactions.

By taking a deeper look into how the LM can assist you with relationship management, you can gain a better appreciation for the LM in general and how you can get more out of your relationships. We will look at the people, processes, and technologies that make up a strong relationship management system.

People

How much time or energy do you spend on getting to know the people with whom you interact on a routine basis? I am not just talking about knowing their names and a few tidbits about their professional and personal lives. I am talking about knowing what makes them tick. Do you understand their role in relation to their organizational mission? Do you know who works with them to accomplish the mission at hand? Do you know their individual and team goals? If they report directly to you, hopefully the answer is yes to these questions and these subjects are discussed routinely as well as during performance counseling. The goal is to have an appropriate understanding of all the people with whom you interact. The following is just a sample of the type of information you should maintain on the people with whom you have a relationship. Use your best judgment as to the level of detail that is appropriate based on the extent of your relationship.

- General Information – Name, organization, title, contact information.

- Category – Personal, co-worker, associate, customer.
- Personal Background – Marriage status, family members, hobbies.
- Professional Background – Education, history, current role, goals.
- Last time you talked to them.
- Rate (between 1 – 10, with 10 being the best) your knowledge of the individual against how well you think you should know that person.

Processes

Think of processes from two perspectives. What processes are in place to facilitate your getting to know the individual better? Also, what COI processes are you and the individual involved in together?

As a leader, you have the ability to influence people with whom you have contact regardless of your formal role or position. Based on this knowledge, you should look at what opportunities you have to strengthen your relationships with people. Some of these may be formal, such as quarterly performance counseling sessions, but most of the opportunities to strengthen your relationship with others will come in more informal settings. These settings include: organizational seminars or ceremonial settings, coffee breaks, meals, or even encounters in the hallway. Recognizing that these are all opportunities to get to know individuals better, it behooves you to be prepared to take advantage of these opportunities. By periodically reviewing the information you have on individuals and keeping notes, you can be better prepared to take your relationship to the next level when the opportunity presents itself.

The second aspect of process regards the information you should collect as you are getting to know the individual better. Specifically, what are the processes in which both of you are involved? Knowing that you both are involved in several organizational processes will help you to frame your relationship. This will enable you to gain a deeper understanding of that person and their roles with respect to the mission. Your knowledge of their role enables a win-win scenario that capitalizes on their expertise. When you are seeking other perspectives to help you reach a decision or gather information for analysis it is your understanding of the individual's expertise that gets you the right person for the task. When you consider principles 2 and 3 of the LM, you can see how valuable it is to not only know the process itself but the people involved.

Technology

There are many different technologies available to help you manage your various relationships. There are many software programs for customer relations management that can assist you. Additionally, most calendar capabilities provide you the ability to manage your contacts. As discussed in Chapter 5, the technology is an enabler to help you accomplish the task at hand. Find one that you are comfortable with and that is adaptable to sharing information and working collaboratively. As you can imagine, much of the information that will help you take your relationship to the next level is already available within your organization's corporate data. Your ability to get to the information and use it productively to build the strong relationships that you seek is where technology can be very helpful.

Relationship Building — A Leader's Perspective

A common mistake among those who work in sports is spending a disproportional amount of time on "x's and o's" as compared to time spent learning about people. - Mike Krzyzewski

To be an effective leader you must first come to the realization that the individuals on your team are the key to success. As indicated by the quote above from Coach Mike Krzyzewski, men's basketball coach at Duke University since 1980, he understands the importance of his players. His success ultimately comes down to his players' ability to perform on the basketball court, not his knowledge of the game. This realization has contributed to teams he has coached winning four NCAA basketball championships and an Olympic gold medal. You can have the greatest plan and even be a good communicator (we will talk more about communication shortly) but if, as a team, you cannot produce results it is all for naught. As you are now familiar with the LM, you notice that we have always placed people ahead of process and technology. There is a reason for that— the LM recognizes the importance of people. Your role as a leader/manager within your COIs requires that you interact with people and recognize that they are the key ingredient. To set them and the team up for success you must know their strengths and weaknesses. In other words, you must have a relationship with them.

Until you understand what is important to them and what makes them tick, you can only motivate or inspire them to a certain degree. It is a thorough understanding of each of them as individuals that enables you as a leader to create an environment for individual and team success. Using a more traditional, stereotypical hierarchical view, we could classify the people we interact with on a professional basis in one of three categories:

- Subordinate – An individual who works for you and is considered to have less responsibility than you. Sometimes, unfortunately, their opinion may not be considered as valuable.
- Contemporary – An individual whose role is considered to be of equal responsibility. They feel more open to provide opinions and views.
- Superior – An individual whose role is considered to have more responsibility. They may feel obligated to share their opinion based on their role.

Often the most productive relationships tend to lean toward the contemporary classification. This type of relationship normally lends itself to open dialogue and enables you to gain a deeper understanding of each other. Don't get me wrong; there are circumstances when approaches that are closer to the other two types of relationships are appropriate. The key to having the strongest relationship possible is to lean toward the contemporary and be cognizant of the situation to recognize when it is appropriate to act otherwise. The leaders who do not have to rely on posi-

> **Your role as a leader/manager within your COIs requires that you interact with people and recognize that they are the key ingredient.**

tion or rank to lead tend to do this. Weaker leaders tend to overvalue themselves and devalue subordinates— often relying on their position or rank as the reason they are "right" when in a disagreement with subordinates.

A weak leader needs status to lead and often the result of this method is that they don't understand their people. The relationships they have with people are hollow. This lack of understanding prevents these leaders from getting the most from their team. What if you are not a "people person" but hold a formal leadership position? You should treat this like any of your other weaknesses and focus on how you can improve it. The beauty of the LM is that it helps you identify your strengths and weaknesses and methodically address your weaknesses.

During my career, I worked for many leaders. Not all of them were naturally comfortable interacting with people. Although many of the best leaders I served for were extroverted and enjoyed working with people, I also served for a few introverts. I once worked for two introverts back to back. Both were similar in that they were quiet and unassuming. Neither felt that they had to force personal interaction with the more junior leaders. Although it appeared that neither enjoyed public speaking or interacting with people, my first boss (Boss One) surely handled the responsibility a lot better than my second (Boss Two). I think the reason Boss One was able to do a better job building relationships is that he recognized the importance of relationships and leading on principle, not position. Although their personalities were similar, Boss One went out of this way to make sure that he did what needed to be done to gain a deeper understanding of the strengths and weaknesses of his leadership team. Boss Two almost went out of his way to avoid interacting with people, particularly individuals who may not agree with his decisions. He was hesitant to commit to any proactive action and preferred sitting in his office talking to a few select people versus going out and "seeing the troops." Similarly, instead of working out differences with his contemporaries, he would instead make his boss aware of the situation and ask him to resolve the problem. His avoidance to interact went as far as avoiding eye contact in the hallway. His discomfort interacting with people on divisive issues never enabled him to get to know his leadership team or give us the opportunity to better understand him. The interactions we had were awkward and not normally productive. Boss One, on the other hand, was able to use his introverted personality traits as an asset in helping build his relationships.

Unlike Boss Two, Boss One had a talent of stimulating conversation and even debate within the group and then he would be able to sit back and listen to the different perspectives that would result from the conversation. He always encouraged different views and was patient in letting individuals get issues off their chest. He had a real talent in doing this. As we would discuss the issues, he would make notes that would help organize the positive and negative aspects of the issue at hand. When the time was right, he would respectfully sum up the discussion and present the information in a manner that normally had everyone in agreement with a path forward. This sounds easy but it is truly a talent that enabled him to gain a better understanding of each individual and bring everyone together on potentially divisive issues. Over time, Boss One created a strong relationship with his team and was very well respected. Even if you did not agree with his decision, the fact that he took the time to communicate why he made the decision he made enabled us to gain a better understanding of his reasoning and of him as a person. His approach facilitated a strong relationship by creating opportunities for all parties involved to gain a better understanding of each other. He created an environment that encouraged open communication and this in turn helped the organization to work together as a team at a very high level of competence.

Communications – The Core of Relationship Building

Communication does not always occur naturally, even among a tight-knit group of individuals. Communication must be taught and practiced in order to bring everyone together as one. - Mike Krzyzewski

As we discussed in Chapter 3, trust is the foundation of a relationship. Trust is built over time and is the result of open and honest communication. Your ability to effectively communicate with people is the only way you can build a relationship. Communications is a powerful skill that requires focused energy to master. Unfortunately, many leaders underestimate the importance of communication and the impact it has on their team and the relationships they are trying to build. An increased awareness in communication will facilitate developing strong relationships faster than you ever imagined. The results of those relationships will enhance your performance and everyone else's within each of your COIs.

There are several aspects of communication that you must appreciate to build strong relationships. First, recognize that communication is most effective when it is going in both directions. You must be able to identify with the other party's perspective in order to effectively communicate and build a strong relationship. This is done by listening to them and taking the time to research what is important to them. This sounds simple, but many people do not take the time to gain an appreciation for what is important to the other person. This is particularly important in the early stages of the relationship when you do not know much about the other person and the foundation of trust has not been well established.

Consider the following illustration. Jim is a personal financial advisor. He has done this for 10 years and has successfully built a strong business. During the last two years, however, he noticed a decline in new-client business. He grows concerned enough to have a business consultant (Susan) look into his situation.

Susan looks into Jim's processes and technologies related to how he brings new clients into his network. On the surface it looks like he has used the same model for a considerable amount of time. His technology is up to date and he uses it well to manage the basic client and financial information he has accumulated over the years. As Susan is working she overhears Jim making a lunch appointment with a prospective new client. Susan later asks if she can join Jim. The following day they meet the prospect (Harry). Jim has made arrangements at a restaurant that he frequents and is very familiar with the menu. He is so familiar, in fact, that he orders for all three as soon as the waiter arrives, suggesting that "you have to try the lasagna because it is the best in the town."

While we are waiting for the meal, Jim quickly jumps into advising Harry where to put his money, what to do in terms of kids' colleges, and even where to retire. If Susan didn't know better she would have thought Jim knew Harry well. Several times, Harry tried to reference his life and his financial concerns; however, Jim didn't seem to care or listen to Harry. By the end of the meal Harry thanks Jim and says he must think about his options. The following day, when Jim calls Harry back, Harry informs Jim that he has decided to go in another direction. Jim tells Susan that Harry doesn't understand the mistake he is making. Susan then asks Jim how he would know given he doesn't know or understand Harry's situation.

It is obvious in the story above that Jim never took the time to get to know Harry or the particulars of his life before advising him. You may not think you act as presumptuous as Jim did but sometimes, when we know a subject better than anyone else in the COI, we tend to think our approach is the right one for any situation and forget to listen to the unique aspects of the situation. Even if you already know the answer, often the other person wants to have the opportunity to express their perspective. We must remind ourselves that listening is an integral part of communications.

While you gain a better understanding of the other person or persons with whom you want a relationship, you should also be communicating what is important to you. This is done by providing a clear, concise message of your point of view. Be consistent with your message. Your goal should be that anyone who knows you knows what to expect from you. Consistency helps you establish solid relationships that are pre-

> **An increased awareness in communication will allow you to develop strong relationships faster than you ever imagined.**

dictable to the other party. A principle-based message of what you stand for also will help you establish a reputation. The old adage "your reputation precedes you" is certainly applicable here. It is your reputation that will allow for quicker and stronger relationship development opportunities. With any relationship expect disagreement in some areas. Be committed to working through those differences by keeping communication lines open. Often, disagreement will initially lead to strained communication. You must be able to respect the fact that we all have opinions and not all our opinions need to be the same. The true test of your leadership ability and the strength of your relationship will come from being able to communicate during these tougher times to create a resolution that hopefully will benefit everyone involved. Complete agreement on the decision or actions that need to take place is not necessary but you cannot afford to have individuals going in the other direction or undermining the decision of the leader. Communicating effectively includes being able to keep everyone focused during times of disagreement. The LM provides a mechanism to facilitate communication and keep the appropriate focus on people using technology to execute a process. The cyclic nature of the LM with such approaches as the recurring azimuth check assessment creates productive communication opportunities.

Many reading this book have likely participated in professional development seminars designed to enhance communication within groups. These seminars point out the importance of communication within your organization and cover many of the points we have discussed not just in this chapter, but within this entire book. There are different exercises to help reinforce the message. One particular exercise deals with how communication gets distorted as it passes through a chain of people who repeat the message they were told to the next person, and so on for five or ten different people. At the end, everyone is amazed at how a simple one- or two-sentence message can become distorted as it passes from one person to the next.

The LM relies on two-way communication to be successful. As we have discussed from a few different perspectives, the LM requires you as a leader to communicate a message to your team. Your team provides you feedback that is organized and focused on performance as individuals and as a team. This feedback is used to continually analyze the people, processes, and technology involved with the mission at hand. You can imagine, and have probably witnessed, what happens when the communication is unclear, inaccurate, or just plain nonexistent.

There are many examples of unclear or lack of communication hurting an organization. Let me draw from many of my experiences in helping organizations with business proposals to create a typical scenario. More often than not, when large organizations provide a proposal for a large contract they have a team of people working to assemble a written document that answers all the requirements outlined in the client's request for proposal (RFP). Here is one situation related to how a proposal manager sets expectations for key interactions within the proposal team.

Tom, the proposal manager, assembles his team for a kick-off meeting. He has assigned writers and subject matter experts (SME) to each section of the proposal. The idea is for the SMEs to provide the technical expertise and the writers to capture that expertise in a manner compliant with the RFP instructions and provide a compelling argument for why the client should hire this company as opposed to others. So the SMEs provide the details of how to solve the client's problems (to include great stories of past successes) and the writers provide the knowledge and skill to best assemble and present the information to the audience.

During the kick-off meeting, Tom takes the time to discuss the importance of the interaction of the SMEs and the writers. He uses a story to communicate how important it is for an effective SME-writer relationship to exist. Tom talks about how when he was a writer in charge of a technical section related to a subject of which he knew little, and was unable to get the SMEs to effectively communicate how they would implement a training program. Tom would ask the SMEs questions and the SMEs' answers almost always would be "that information is within the documents I already provided you." That was accurate; however, the SMEs had provided dozens of documents, many of which were hundreds of pages. The bottom line was that Tom was drowning in information but what he needed was knowledge— the knowledge that the SMEs had in their heads. The SMEs could easily and quickly find answers to questions and, more importantly, understood many of the hidden challenges in the requirements that Tom would never be able to understand because he did not have experience specific to that area. Tom ultimately assembled his section and it was compliant, providing the information required. However, what it lacked was a compelling argument demonstrating a thorough understanding of the client's requirements and the offeror's knowledge in how to solve problems that can be expected in the effort.

Tom's story communicated his expectation of the SME-writer relationship. He further discussed how he would review sections with the SME-writer team to identify strengths and weaknesses of their written products. Tom would review the work with both and at the end each would know what actions needed to be accomplished to get the section ready to submit to the client. Tom has effectively communicated what is expected of the SME-writer team and how he will provide feedback through reviews. Everyone now knows what their role is and what is expected of them.

Clear communication and constant monitoring is paramount to avoid false expectations and an environment filled with inaccurate or missing information. Like anything in life, to be good at something you need to do it often. For this reason, the LM provides a foundation for setting up continual feedback mechanisms. Using the LM, you and your team establish appropriate formal and informal feedback mechanisms to provide constant interaction among everyone within the organization and the larger COI. These interactions will provide the much needed communication to build productive and quality relationships.

Conclusion

In this chapter we took the LM and looked at it from a slightly different perspective. We focused on the synergy that comes from thinking about the importance that relationships provide for you to be efficient and effective in your mission. Organizations require teamwork to succeed. Relationships are the underpinnings of good teamwork. We specifically discussed how awareness of people, process, and technology within the LM can be used to facilitate your ability to create and manage strong and productive relationships.

As a leader/manager, it is important for you to recognize successful approaches to build and sustain relationships. The essence of a strong relationship is built through communication. These relationships provide opportunities for individuals and teams to become better in performing their mission and recognize unrealized potential for the future. The following table highlights some of the benefits related to leadership/ management and to the organization as a whole and considers the key concepts discussed in this chapter. Following the table, I asked Fran Trentley, Senior Service Line Director, Public Sector, Akamai, the industry leader in content delivered through the internet, to share his views related to relationships and the concepts discussed in this chapter.

Key concepts and benefits to you as a leader and to the organization	
Relationship management and the LM – a simple approach to enhance awareness	
Benefits to the Leader/Manager:	Benefits to the Organization:
• Use a people, processes, and technology approach to enhance your relationships	• This approach aligns with recurring azimuth checks and personnel performance systems for focus
Relationship building – a leader's perspective	
Benefits to the Leader/Manager:	Benefits to the Organization:
• Recognize that people will act based on the type of relationship they have with you	• An organization's performance can change based on the leader's ability to build relationships
Communications – the core of relationship building	
Benefits to the Leader/Manager:	Benefits to the Organization:
• Encouraging open and honest communications strengthens relationships	• Maximizes the development of individuals and provides the foundation for continued improvement

Fran Trentley and I have a personal and professional relationship going back to 1998, when we both attended the Army Command and General Staff College. I have always admired Fran's ability to build and maintain strong relationships that enable him to build win-win situations for everyone he works with. As you read Fran's input to this chapter I think it best exemplifies that you can be yourself and create your own leadership philosophy for success. Fran is very much atypical in his approach to successfully lead people. Even within his unique style, which consistently produces the best from his teams, he remains consistent to the principles within the LM that we have discussed throughout this book. Now Fran provides his thoughts on the importance of building and maintaining strong relationships and how the concepts within this chapter can help individuals and organizations foster such relationships. Enjoy Fran's contributions to the subject; I did.

Ed Zimmerman

Creating Productive Relationships

Q. Please share your thoughts on the importance of building and maintaining professional relationships.

Fortunately, I can exclude relationships with one's God, family, 'significant other,' and one's self and stick to professional relationships. That said, even professional relationships are a broad subject and have had quite a bit of study dedicated to them by men far wiser than I. What I think is this: Professional relationships are good and you should get some and keep them.

At the core of every relationship is a belief in mutual betterment. In more basic terms, what we like to call a win-win. Our relationship with our God will bring us salvation, our relationship with our family will bring us joy and immortality, and our expectation is that our professional relationships will bring us mutual success. Why else would you have them unless you're self-destructive or extremely generous? You are going to meet a lot of people throughout the years; try hard to make friends. I know people that are just natural extroverts and do this very well; I'm not. To be honest, I don't waste time on the people I don't like, I'll never develop long-term relationships with them, and I enjoy interacting with friends more. As you get to be old like me you understand the need to keep in touch with friends that you've made throughout your life. Not that I send Christmas cards (I don't) but I do try to make it a habit to call now and again to see how things are going. Every friendship makes your team stronger.

There is no better way to solve a problem than to assemble your own think tank. Being able to link requirements with resources is the key to maintaining strong relationships. Your friends should know that if they need an arc-welder this weekend that you probably know someone who has one. When you need a contact in the Canadian government you should know who to call that has one. If you're looking for personnel or someone needs help putting a proposal together at the last minute... you get this idea. No one succeeds as an individual for long.

Q. As a leader, what characteristics do you think are the most important in building relationships with subordinates, contemporaries, and superiors?

Strong relationships are built on underlying mutual respect and expectation of support. I do not distinguish among the respect you extend to subordinates, peers, or superiors because those are role definitions and determine expectations of knowledge, skills, and abilities and determine responsibility and scope of accountability. Roles should not determine level of respect. Roles will constantly change throughout all of our lives but relationships should remain consistent. Respect is contagious and will spread throughout your team as quickly as a lack thereof. This is the key... pay attention.

I've been around the block once or twice and have seen my peers in the same moment be courteous to me while in almost in the same breath rude to a subordinate. I have had a superior officer use me as you would an "implement" or a weapon instead of a teammate. I later turned down a command where I would have reported to this same officer. Trust me; it makes a difference in your individual performance and that of the team. I would be willing to bet that with very little introspection you could think of identical situations in your own careers.

I address my customers, my peers, my superiors, and the wonderful people that I have the responsibility to lead as Sir or Ma'am. You should too.

Q. Are there any specific processes or technology you use to help you manage your relationships?

There are tools that will help you if you care and make the effort. There are a ton of applications that are available; I make moderate use of LinkedIn. There are so many of these types of tools out there you just need to identify, preferably collaboratively within the team, which one you're all going to use and stick with it. I use a custom tool called the long commute. It works like this: first, spend a couple hours every day driving to and from work; then, call people and catch up during the long commute. It works well for me as a rule, but every once in a while someone will be traveling and I'll catch them at 3 a.m.... still fun though.

Q. Based on your experience, what techniques do you use to facilitate communication within your team? Please share an example of how improved communications helped solve a problem or contributed to an improvement.

I am an extremely open, honest, and loud over-communicator. I believe the key to success is to ensure everyone understands what is expected of them and what they should expect of me. You should never be in a position where you can't communicate openly with your team leaders or personnel. I have developed a mantra that has served me well for many years:
• No individual more important than the team

- No team more important than the mission
- No mission more important than mine!

It has been well communicated and clear in every one of the teams that I will absolutely get rid of an individual that is negatively impacting the team. I will absolutely get rid of an entire team that is undermining the mission and there is no more important mission than the mission that I am assigned. I expect all my people to try their best; I expect them to be professional and I expect them to be successful. I encourage them to hold me to the same standard and call me out if I am found wanting. Yes, my team has the right to "vote me off the island."

One more thing: set the example, take responsibility, and be accountable. You communicate more to your team and your friends through actions than words. I attempt to instill in my leaders that they shouldn't judge people (to include me) by what they say; it's actions that define them. Watch what they do.

I know this will sound counter intuitive but you have to keep it fun! "Why, you old softy…" you say. "No," I say and I'll tell you why. No one likes coming to a miserable work place, and they won't for long. No one will recommend that their "wicked" smart friends come to work in a hell hole. No one likes calling the "boss" if it is painful every time they do. I, on more than one occasion, have briefed my team that "I don't take care of you because I love you, I take care of you because I want to squeeze the maximum productivity out of you and I can't do that if you're worried about mama or the kids. I want work to be your favorite thing to do and place to go." This doesn't mean that you don't maintain high standards and high expectations. This just means you can't be an overbearing jerk while doing it.

I had the opportunity to be "rewarded" with an exceptionally low score on a new "experimental" metric a while back. Now, to set the stage, let it be known that my team consistently "rocks the house" on all metrics and measures so this gave my "loving" peers and superiors great joy and they took every opportunity to bust my chops about it. I took it all in stride and told them three things. First, this was absolutely my responsibility; second, that I would fix it; and third, that the next quarter I would have the highest scores in the organization.

My team knows they rock but were absolutely embarrassed about letting their boss get the razzing for this. They hold themselves to a much higher standard than I could ever justify… but that didn't save them from what they would call the "rant." It went something like this… "the organization doesn't need us to get a score like this… in fact, they may have done better without us here 'helping' them… do you know I had to raise my hand and say "Yes sir, that was me that got that score and it won't happen again" in an open forum! I don't care what we have to do blah blah... (played on volume 11) we will have the top score in the organization next quarter or your next boss will be even meaner than me."

So yes. I like to be dramatic at times and play the guilt card and in this particular case they know me well so it probably had no effect on the outcome. In the next quarter we had the highest score in the company's history. It was nearly perfect... and I complained about that, too.

Q. Finally, as you look back in your professional and personal life, share any final thoughts you have related to leadership/management and the impact it has had on your life.

I think my own understanding of the traits that I reinforced in my own personality come with time and introspection. If you had asked me why I was successful as a young lieutenant, when I was a young lieutenant, I would have told you simply, "Sleep last, eat last, work the hardest, and make on-the-spot corrections." I would have told you that rewards are for your men/women and your team needs to be the best at marksmanship, physical training, and land navigation. Now just go do it.

A few years later I would have given you a more complete answer. I would have added that you need to identify that one amazing, first ever, new capability thing that the team can accomplish as a goal. I would love for you to believe I knew this all the time but to be honest, I did this either by accident or because we came up with it as a team. Probably on one of those sleep-deprived evenings when someone says "Wouldn't it be cool if we could." From Jim Collins' book *Good to Great*... figure what you can be the best at and go do it. I also would have added that you need to know your people.

When I was a commander, I had responsibility for 170 young men and women. I knew them all by name on sight, but more I understood their personalities and strengths. I have always played to my people's strengths. I had a young man in my troop that was borderline firing material. A real pain in the rear, he was disrespectful, undisciplined, and a drag on the morale of the unit. Unfortunately, he also was bright, a natural leader, and technically proficient. Some in the unit were drawn to him like flies. So I had a decision to make, and I did; I gave him additional responsibility. I put him in charge of tasks with soldiers to guide.

Worked like a champ; the change was noticeable in weeks, and he became a valued member of the team. I learned a lesson at that point: natural leadership can be used for good or evil, you need to direct it. I tried this "trick" again on a few occasions throughout my career; sometimes it worked and sometimes it reinforced another lesson. You have to groom the team.

Brigadier General Thomas E. Swain was the Deputy Assistant Secretary of Defense for Special Operations and Low-Intensity Conflict (Policy and Missions) when he retired in 1996. Ten years earlier he was a Colonel and Commander of the 25th Infantry Division (Light), Division Artillery. I was a scrappy lieutenant in the 3/7 Field Artillery, a battalion under COL Swain's command. COL Swain was as hard as woodpecker lips and his command philosophy was the first I had ever seen as a young officer. It also is the best I have seen since. It addressed loyalty and duty and was extremely direct and pointed. To this day I remember verbatim the edict to make on-the-spot corrections: "If you overlook poor performance you set a new standard of excellence." I drive this point home with all my teams.

As a leader you have the responsibility to keep the team healthy. Recognize and reward outstanding performance, train and develop good performers, and recognize and remove substandard performers. I have never been in a leadership position where I have not been forced to fire someone for the good of the team. Don't think for a minute that it's pleasant or that it gets easier with time or experience, but you have to cull the herd, as it were, and I can promise you that you won't have to guess who has to go. They will make themselves very apparent and do everything but stand up and yell "Fire me!"

I have been extremely fortunate to lead high performance teams throughout my military career and I have been blessed with the team I have been assigned in my current organization. I always try to remember that I am as much here for them as they are for me. I let this philosophy guide my decisions and I try not to forget the first rule.

The first rule of successful relationships and building high performance teams is to remember that you need a team to be successful. The day you forget that and start to believe you got where you are by yourself, and that you alone accomplished great things, is when you fail to succeed. Don't get too big for your britches.

Knives do not a chef make— a favorite with professional chefs, Japanese knife companies produce some very functional, high quality knives. The forged stainless steel blades are extremely sharp and perfectly balanced. My mother is the best cook I ever met and should have her own show. She uses a 70-year-old knife that belonged to her mother and it's been sharpened so many times it barely qualifies as a knife anymore.

The techniques I've talked about are like my mother's knife; they work for me and "fit" my disposition and personality. Take the time to find your own knife; you might not be happy with mine.

Ed's Final Thoughts

Having worked with Fran, and also carpooled with him during two separate assignments in the Army, I know him well. I have seen him build teams and make them top performers. We have discussed personal and professional subjects for many hours while we sat in a car together commuting to and from work. My observations are that people feel compelled to perform their best for him. His openness, his dedication to excellence, and his willingness to promote a team environment endear him to them. You could call him "Firm but Fair Fran," and I think that most people who work for a leader who is firm but fair respect that and ultimately enjoy that environment. You always know what to expect and that is a key to success, as well as to happiness.

Chapter 8

Opportunity -
Yours Could Be Right in Front of You

*We are all faced with a series of great opportunities brilliantly disguised
as impossible situations.*
- Charles R. Swindoll

Opportunities come far more often than we realize. We are so accustomed to living within our daily routine that when we face a situation outside of that environment we fail to recognize it as an opportunity to grow in some fashion. Just having awareness of this fact can enable us to take advantage of these situations. The LM acts as a paradigm for how you conduct yourself within your relationships and can help you recognize the opportunities as they present themselves. The best leaders have built strong relationships that help them influence people up, down, and across organizational or COI lines. This influence is what sustains current relationships and leads to future opportunities. Future opportunities enable an organization to grow stronger and more influential.

The systematic approach provided by the LM creates opportunities by taking advantage of open communications to develop strong relationships that foster innovation and change. Ideas are exchanged between leaders and their teams. Best practices are measured and refined. Individuals are empowered with knowledge and developed for future challenges. These are all examples of opportunities for the organization to become better. The LM provides a model that addresses today's performance as well as opportunities for future success.

Many of these opportunities come from what on the surface may appear as a failure. It is important to recognize that when you create an environment that promotes aggressively looking for ways to improve your organization and how you perform your mission there are bound to be short-term failures. When we talked about empowerment, we discussed how a leader's reaction to adverse situations plays a significant role in whether or not individuals will be willing to take the risk to get out of their comfort zone. A leader who creates an opportunistic mindset will be able to move past short-term failures and turn what appears to be a negative situation into a positive one.

An Opportunistic Mindset – Creating Opportunities

When one door of happiness closes, another opens; but often we look so long at the closed door that we do not see the one which has been opened for us. - Helen Keller

Everyday opportunities come to us but we don't recognize them. We are too caught up in our daily routine to appreciate the opportunities that present themselves to us. As we discussed in Chapter 6, at least part of the reason is that we spend so much time and energy working insignificant issues that we don't recognize opportunities when they emerge. If we do recognize an opportunity, often we are not prepared to take advantage of it.

To help you take advantage of opportunities, the LM helps you identify them and enables you to be prepared to act on them. The LM creates an opportunistic mindset by taking a methodical approach to identifying opportunities. By making this a part of your daily operating procedures, you will be ready when opportunities come.

In the macro, the second and third principles of the LM provide a continuous cycle of looking at how to improve your people, processes, and/or technology. Informally we, as leaders, should be looking for opportunities by thinking in terms of the continuous cycle of communicating, planning, executing, monitoring, and providing feedback. This informal continuous thought process provides the real-time awareness of what is going on within your areas of responsibility. The knowledge that is created and shared lends itself to a constant preparedness for overcoming bad situations and for taking advantage of opportunities that present themselves. These opportunities may be small tweaks in how you use a team member's knowledge or skill to better serve the team or fix a broken process. It may be that you can eliminate a process altogether as a result of a new technology. These are examples of small opportunities that present themselves routinely when you are in touch with how the people, processes, and technologies interact within your organization or COIs.

On a larger scale, we should be continually looking at how the results of our team provide a service or product to our customer. Using our azimuth check assessment as a more formal means to look for opportunities we institutionalize the LM mindset for continual improvement. Ultimately, you start by understanding your customers' needs and looking at how to make them more efficient and effective. When you look at opportunities strategically, the best thing you can do is provide your customer a capability that makes their life easier and more productive. This

> Using our azimuth check assessment as a more formal means to look for opportunities we institutionalize the LM mindset for continual improvement.

comes from thoroughly understanding your customers' perspectives and a relationship with your customers that facilitate your ability to solve their problems.

This sounds too simple, doesn't it? Sometimes the opportunities to create a positive impact are very simple, they just need someone who can act on them and be willing to support the change needed. This book is filled with examples of opportunities to make a difference and the people who were involved either acted or they didn't. I am sure you can think of many situations that you have faced when someone acted or didn't act on an opportunity. When I think of opportunities, I quickly think of the entrepreneurs and how aggressive they are in seeking and moving on opportunities.

Richard W. Sears (co-founder and first President of Sears and Roebuck) comes to mind. In 1886, as a station agent for the Minneapolis and St. Louis Railroad, Sears took advantage of the opportunity that was right in front of him. As a railroad agent, time was an important element of information. Sears recognized this and the fact that he and other agents would want to have a reliable watch to keep accurate time. He acquired a small stockpile of watches from a manufacturer and then used the railroad system to sell and distribute watches to other agents who needed this technology to perform their job.

At 22, and six months after he started selling watches, he resigned from the railroad and started building what would eventually turn into Sears and Roebuck. He started by just selling watches and using the railroad system to distribute these watches. His foresight in providing mail-order catalogs and using the railroad system for distribution was instrumental in building one of the most successful companies our country has ever seen. In the early 1900's more than 50,000 house assembly kits were sold and shipped via the railroad. The mail-order shipping business continued to grow for decades as Sears and Roebuck continued to expand. The company produced a general catalog until 1993. This success all started with Richard Sears having an awareness of the opportunities in front of him. What opportunities are in front of you right now?

Take the time to look carefully because too often one man's opportunity is viewed as a waste of time to another. This is why you need to look at these in an educated, methodical manner, which is in essence what the LM enables you to do. If you are not prepared for the opportunity when it comes then it is not an opportunity for you. Be ready and seize the moment.

My development of the LM and this book are a result of being prepared to act on an opportunity that supported my passion. The LM was not developed overnight. I had been collecting my thoughts and studying the dynamics of this for many years before formalizing this concept. During my last five years in the Army, I had started to really put some thought to many of the concepts that I have summed up within the LM. After I retired from the Army, my experience running a small IT company for a year provided a transition for me to start my consulting company. As a consultant, I have been fortunate to work with many large and small companies involved in many different business sectors. This consulting experience helped solidify, in my mind, that a framework, such as the LM, can be a valuable tool for any leader who is seeking opportunities for improvement. I employ the use of the LM in either a formal or informal fashion for every consulting job I perform. My use of the LM in these settings helps me provide my client an improvement opportunity while also providing me the opportunity to further refine the LM concept for future use. This is a true win-win situation.

It is important to note that these opportunities for improvement almost always were a result of collaborative efforts from a group of people. Rarely have I found that opportunities present themselves and can be seized without other people playing a role. One of the primary reasons is that often the opportunity cannot be recognized and solved without alternative views or perspectives for consideration. This goes back to our introduction of this section and the quote from Helen Keller. Next time a door closes spend less time looking at that closed door and more time focusing your team on the door that opened.

Become a Great Leader/Manager: What Are You Waiting For?

Opportunities multiply as they are seized. - Sun Tzu

We have emphasized that opportunities come in many fashions. Success stimulates more opportunity and from what can appear to be a failure opportunity also exists. The key is maintaining a situational awareness that enables you to recognize the opportunity and be prepared to capitalize on that opportunity. As you come to the end of the book an opportunity to improve yourself as a person and a leader now exists. This book has provided you with a perspective to consider how you conduct yourself in the different roles of your life. Are you going to seize the opportunity? The Leadership Map can be interpreted as a guide to help you discover the opportunities that exist within your organization and within your life. I challenge you to seek areas of improvement. Identify small habits that you can improve on and start making those changes.

Now is a great time for you to reflect on who you are and how you serve as a leader/manager within the daily context of your life. First, you must take the time to define the different roles you serve. I recommend you prioritize your roles within the various COIs and start with the most important roles. Define your role and develop goals to support continual improvement. Map them to the greater purpose (mission and vision). When a formal organization exists, take the time to learn the organizational structure and the roles within. This sounds like a lot of work but really it is not. The information is all around you; all you need to do is organize it. The time will be well spent, as it will help you prioritize what you work on daily and get you out of working in a crisis action mode and working more strategically. Wouldn't it be nice to start the day already knowing on what you want to focus your energy? Try taking just ten minutes at the end of the day to make your "to do list" for the following day. Review it

> **The key is maintaining a situational awareness that allows you to recognize the opportunity and be prepared to capitalize on that opportunity.**

first thing in the morning and think about how you will accomplish it during your commute. You will be surprised what a large impact such a small change can have in your life. What would you like accomplished in the next week— month— year? Imagine the impact on your life as a whole if you were to start institutionalizing the concepts we discussed in the book.

Armed with your roles and goals, you can start employing the principles of the LM. You first gain an understanding of the people, processes, and technologies that exists in every function for which you are involved (principle 1). Now systematically exercise the basic LM cycle:

- Communicate, inspire, and empower your team
- Plan and execute
- Monitor and measure results
- Provide feedback, inspire, and empower to improve and optimize
- Continually repeat the process informally as you assess daily activities
- Use the azimuth check assessment as a formal means to ensure you stay on course
  Going through this LM cycle you and your team are looking for ways to support the second and third principles of the LM that will ultimately improve your performance and provide future opportunities.

- Principle 2— Continual navigation involving people, processes, and technology leads to improvement.
- Principle 3— A direction change in people, processes, or technology requires an azimuth check of the other two.

Your awareness related to performance and continual improvement will be directly related to your consistency in using a LM mindset. This increased awareness will enable you to become more in tune to the key characteristics of people, processes, and technology that we have discussed in this book. You and your organization will start to operate using a different paradigm that promotes a proactive approach, which creates a synergy of a well-balanced team. The LM approach will provide strategic value, creating strong relationships and future opportunities. In fact, your relationships will facilitate opportunities. Opportunities will stimulate more relationships that can be further developed. This revolving door concept enables you to continually grow individually and gives your organization a chance to become better in the future.

What kind of improvements are we talking about? And how will those improvements lead to opportunities?

- Focusing your energy to achieve specific goals – the focus will increase your awareness of what is required to achieve the goal and opportunities will become more obvious.
- Ability to see issues from other perspectives – enabling you to think of alternative solutions that you would not have seen before.
- Provide the confidence to make bold decisions and navigate through the challenges associated with that decision – venture into markets you once feared were too tough for you.
- Embrace change as a way of life, continually seeking personal improvement – a better, more purposeful life with the satisfaction that comes with success and continual improvement.

As you take advantage of this opportunity to enhance your skills as a leader/manager, you may find that it takes some time to get comfortable with the LM. Remember, you are trying to become a better leader/ manager and you need to give it a chance. Like any change, this does not happen overnight; give it some time. In today's world, technology creates enormous opportunities to move information. Email is a wonderful technology that accommodates quick movement of information— so quick that sometimes we forget that we are dealing with people who can normally more effectively communicate in person. So, as part of your azimuth check assessment program, get out and see people— build relationships. Too many leaders have isolated themselves from the people they lead. You can expect that an effort to get out of the office in more informal interactions with your team will mean that you lose time doing emails and reports and all those other "important things" but the insight you will gain through sincere interactions with your team will outweigh the missed email that was not answered.

The LM will change your perspective on how you view the issues and challenges that you routinely face. You may find that you only want to use some of the techniques from the LM and leave some out. This is all right. A more personalized framework should ultimately be your goal. When you start to increase your awareness as a leader/manager you should have a very personalized approach that takes advantage of your experiences and leads to future opportunities, as well as continued success.

Conclusion

As a leader/manager, you are always seeking opportunities to make you and your organization more efficient and effective. Your ability to take advantage of these opportunities is what will lead to long-term sustained success. Opportunities often exist that we do not recognize; the LM is designed to help you better recognize these opportunities. The following table highlights some of the benefits related to leadership/management, as well as to the organization as a whole, and considers the key concepts discussed in this chapter. Following the table, I have asked Tom Corley to share his views with respect to how important it is to seek and take advantage of life's opportunities. Tom's participation is an example of taking advantage of an opportunity.

Key concepts and benefits to you as a leader and to the organization	
An opportunistic mindset – creating opportunities	
Benefits to the Leader/Manager:	Benefits to the Organization:
• Enables creative opportunities for self improvement and organizational benefit	• Institutionalizes the informal and formal atmosphere to produce opportunities
Become a great leader/manager – what are you waiting for?	
Benefits to the Leader/Manager:	Benefits to the Organization:
• Use the LM concept as an opportunity to evaluate your role and performance	• Create an empowered team able to evaluate their performance and seek future opportunities

Tom Corley is a financial planner, entrepreneur, and author. I met Tom briefly a few years ago. I know his brother, Tim, very well. I think it is appropriate for Tom to be the guest expert in the chapter about opportunity because our collaboration on this endeavor is exactly the type of opportunity I talk about previously and Tom talks about here. Let me share how I came to ask Tom to provide his insight.

As I was assembling my team of guest experts I had all my chapters filled except for this chapter. At the same time, I was looking for more information related to publishing my book. During a conversation with my friend Tim Corley, I mentioned my book and that I was trying to figure out what to do in reference to publishing it. Tim suggested I call his brother, Tom, who recently self-published a book. So I called Tom and we discussed the ups and downs of self-publishing. Of course we discussed his book and my book as well. After our conversation, I ordered and read Tom's book, *Rich Habits*. Not only did I enjoy the book, I could identify with the concepts he presented in his book and how they were very similar to the philosophy that I present in my book, except from more of a personal finance perspective versus a leadership perspective.

After reading Tom's book, I knew I had found the right person to provide the insight on this chapter. Just as I saw this as my opportunity, Tom saw this as an opportunity to further share his insights and promote his book and his business. I cannot think of a more perfect example of two individuals being opportunistic and taking advantage of a situation that presented itself. Now, enjoy Tom's contributions to this chapter.

Opportunities through Rich Habits

Q. Please share your thoughts on the importance of an informal mindset that seeks out opportunities.

Passion is the fuel for uncovering opportunities. Without passion for what you do it is very difficult to see the opportunities that are right before your eyes. Passion energizes your thinking. It opens up your eyes to opportunities. It helps you focus on looking for the solutions to the obstacles that are in your way. You can't teach passion. It is an intangible that is a prerequisite for success in whatever you do. Finding your passion opens up the door to opportunities. Think of passion as your opportunity-seeking missile. If you don't have passion for what you do you will never see the opportunities.

Q. Please share your thoughts on the importance of a formal approach (such as the azimuth check) to seek or create opportunities.

A formal approach to creating opportunity is essential to success. I have captured a couple that, like the LM and the azimuth check, enhance your awareness for the opportunities that present themselves.

#1 Processing the Rich Habits into Your Life

In my role as a CPA and Certified Financial Planner, I help my clients manage their taxes and their wealth and, thus, I am privy to the in-ner workings of the world of the wealthy. In my other role as a financial self-help author I have, through years of research, gained a very unique understanding of how mere mortals create immense wealth. As a consequence of my two roles I am often asked by those struggling financially how the wealthy make their money. I codified these wealth creation activities into what I call "Rich Habits." One of the most profound things that came out of the research for my book was the realization that wealthy people create their own luck by doing specific things, which I call "living the rich habits." By doing these specific things, by living the rich habits, they process luck into their lives. Most wealthy individuals, I found, were not even aware that they were the manufacturers of their own luck. They just thought they were "lucky." Case in point, the late J. Paul Getty, oil tycoon, when asked to what he attributed his immense wealth, he stated: "Some people find oil, others don't." Even Getty thought his wealth was a matter of random luck. For this very reasoning, the concept of creating wealth has been shrouded in mystery. Thus the phrase "the secret to financial success." But thanks to the discoveries I made in my research, the secret to financial success is no longer a secret. The fact is, creating wealth is nothing more than processing success into your lives by living the rich habits and watching opportunity manifest itself out of thin air. Wealthy people, whether they know it or not, are every day manufacturing opportunity luck by the way they live their lives— by their daily habits. Think of opportunity luck as a tree. When you live your life a certain way, when you live the rich habits, you are planting opportunity luck seeds. As you nurture your tree, as you live the rich habits, your opportunity luck tree grows. In time, your opportunity luck tree will bear fruit. Think of this fruit as a manifestation of luck. This fruit may be a raise, a promotion, a bonus, a financial windfall, a long, healthy life, good relationships etc. The Rich Habits:

1. I will form good habits and follow these good habits every day.
2. I will set goals for each day, for each month, for each year and for the long-term. I will focus on my goals each and every day.
3. I will engage in self-improvement every day.
4. I will devote part of each and every day in caring for my health.
5. I will devote each and every day to forming lifelong relationships.
6. I will live each and every day in a state of moderation.
7. I will accomplish my daily tasks each and every day. I will adopt a "do it now" mindset.
8. I will engage in rich thinking every day.
9. I will save 10% of my gross income every paycheck.
10. I will control my thoughts and emotions each and every day.

The key to financial and personal success rests in your daily habits. If you want to be financially successful you need to change your daily habits. You need to eliminate bad habits and replace them with good habits, or what I call rich habits. Living rich habits every day will create the opportunity luck that the wealthy enjoy.

#2 Daily Career-Related Self-Improvement

In my five-year study of the daily success habits of wealthy individuals one important discovery I made was that wealthy individuals are fanatics when it comes to daily career-related self-improvement. The reason? They are in constant pursuit of opportunities to help their customers or clients through value-added services or products. I uncovered four ways that wealthy individuals engage in opportunity-seeking self-improvement: reading, writing, speaking, and doing. Each one gets you higher up the ladder of financial success.

Reading - Many of us get those monthly industry periodicals. Typically, we set them aside and tell ourselves that we will get to that reading very soon. We may even pull out the periodicals, after a week or two, and browse through them, pulling out articles we are intent on reading. We set these articles aside and, again, tell ourselves we will get to that reading very soon. After a few months we throw these periodicals/articles out, rationalizing that they are outdated and of no use. Their time value has rendered them outdated. Wealthy individuals have a different tact. They set aside time every day for reading. They read every one of their periodicals. The reason? Wealthy individuals understand the value of timely information. They are in pursuit of opportunities to make more money. Often these opportunities are contained within the written words inside their industry periodicals. Wealthy individuals will typically set aside 30 to 45 minutes of every day for career-related reading. They do this day in and day out. Wealthy individuals understand that reading helps them remain current with industry technical information and industry trends that might lead to opportunities. To wealthy individuals, reading gets them one rung higher on the ladder of financial success.

Writing - Writing is a form of communication. Because we are writing on a topic, we must gain a better understanding of that topic than simple reading will provide. Writing often requires additional research and a more complex understanding of the topic that is the subject of the writing. Wealthy individuals engage in writing in a number of ways, which include: company newsletters, industry newsletters, newspaper articles, industry publication articles, Internet articles, and customer/client letters. Writing is another rung on the ladder of success, getting you higher up that ladder.

Speaking - Speaking, like writing, is a form of communication. Speaking requires a greater understanding of a subject matter than writing. There is a simple reason for this. In a speaking engagement you may be asked a question. We all have egos. When we are "the expert" on a topic for which we have been asked to speak, our egos are deflated when we are unable to answer a question. The need to really know a topic, for this reason, is much greater in a speaking engagement than it is in writing. Speaking forces you to know your subject matter that much better, and thus elevates you up another rung on the ladder of success.

Doing - There is no better way to perfect your knowledge in an area than through repetition by doing. Repetition in a particular area gets you closer to perfection than reading, writing, or speaking ever could. Each time you repeat a task in a particular area you become more efficient and more expert. Doing, over and over again, enables you to make and fix mistakes and improve and perfect your skill-set. Through repetition by doing you will, in time, become a master in a particular task or subject matter.

The wealthiest of individuals employ all four career-related self-improvement activities. But, in reality, you can achieve financial success by simply dedicating yourself, every day, to just one of the four career-related, self-improvement methods. Make no mistake about it; it's not an easy discipline. Daily career-related self-improvement is boring. It's tedious. But the by-product is uncovering opportunities. Imagine you are standing in a forest. What do you see? You see trees. You see all of the trees that are in front of you. These trees are a metaphor for opportunities. Now imagine off to the side of the forest is a hill. This hill is a metaphor for career-related self-improvement. What happens when you climb that hill (what happens when you engage in daily career-related, self-improvement)? You notice that there are many more trees in the forest (more opportunities). The higher and higher you climb that hill (the more you engage in career-related self-improvement), the more trees you see (the more opportunities you see). The more opportunities you see in your life, the more money you make.

The wealthiest of individuals utilize all four strategies for success, although many focus on only one or two strategies and yet still reap enormous rewards. No one can become financially successful without incorporating one or more of these strategies in their lives. Unsuccessful people do the bare minimum in their careers. They avoid reading, writing, and speaking. They "do" only the bare minimum to keep their job. They are not interested in perfecting their craft or bettering themselves in their profession. They are blind to opportunities. That is too bad. Until you engage in daily career-related self-improvement, you are walking around blind to the multiple opportunities that lie before you and that lift you up the ladder of financial success.

Q. As a leader, what do you think is your role in facilitating opportunities? Can you provide a technique you have used in the past to create an opportunity?

Successful individuals view relationships as if they were gold. Relationships are the currency of the successful. Each relationship you have is like a tree. The size of each one of your relationship trees depends on how much you nurture the relationship. Successful individuals build their relationship trees into redwoods. The byproduct of these strong relationships is the manifestation of opportunities. Your strongest relationships will deliver to you opportunities on a silver platter. Whether through referrals, recommendations, advice or solutions, your strongest relationships constantly feed you with opportunities. How do you strengthen your relationships in order to facilitate opportunities? Successful individuals build relationships using four techniques:

#1 The Hello Call is a simple call you make to your relationships to say hello. But it is much more than that. Think of your hello call as reconnaissance. The purpose of the hello call is to gather information about your relationship. Their birthday, names of family members, college attended, groups or organizations with which they are affiliated, hobbies, and so on. This information is then documented and stored into your relationship's individual database.

#2 The Happy Birthday Call is a call you make once a year to wish your relationship a happy birthday. This call keeps your relationship on life support. It keeps it alive.

#3 The Life Event Call is the most powerful call you can make. A life event call is like putting your relationship tree on steroids. The roots to the tree grow deep after a life event call. Life events include a birth, marriage, graduation, promotion, achievement, and the like.

#4 Group Participation. The last relationship-building technique is participation in groups. Group participation forges bonds that are not easily broken. Whether the group is within your workplace or outside of it, your participation helps to showcase your skill-sets, attitude, work ethic, and personality. Groups bind individuals together. Group participation is invaluable in facilitating opportunities.

Q. Are there any specific processes or technology you use to help you manage opportunities?

Relationship Opportunities

Maintaining a detailed database on all of your relationships helps uncover opportunities with respect to your relationships. The more information you gather on each relationship, the clearer you can see opportunities. These opportunities may be a service or product you recognize your relationship needs or wants. Understanding everything about your relationship helps you to meet these needs and wants. When you passionately focus on the needs and wants of your relationships, opportunities manifest themselves out of thin air. As you gather more information on your relationship you will see these opportunities and can list them in the individual database you maintain for your relationship, whether that is Outlook, Goldmine, Maximizer, or some other database management system.

Technical Opportunities

Daily career-related self-improvement helps improve your technical skills in your career and industry. Writing, seminars, lectures, teaching, or speaking engagements force you to dig deeper into a technical area. Any time you have to communicate, whether in writing or verbally, you must gain a keener understanding of the topic or technical area. You must dig deeper. This digging helps you uncover opportunities, which then become part of your written or verbal communication project/engagement. Articles, presentation material, and written speeches help memorialize the opportunities you uncover in your research and preparation for the writing or speaking engagement. They become part of the project and may be invaluable down the road in leveraging the uncovered opportunity when a need or want of an individual or organization manifests itself.

Q. Finally, as you look back in your professional and personal life, share any final thoughts you have related to leadership/management and the impact it has had on your life.

There is no one template for a leader. Tall, small, fat, thin, black, white, smart, average. It does not matter. Leaders come in many forms and personality types. The one constant in being a leader, I have learned through the years, is risk. Leaders take on risk that others avoid at all costs. Often times a risk event occurs and it is demoralizing. But true leaders understand the risks and expect failures and mistakes. I have seen leaders emerge from the ashes of start-up failures. It is the failures and mistakes from which lessons are best learned and true leadership is forged. The best leaders, I have found, are the ones who have tried and failed. I don't want to follow someone who is successful if they have never failed. Murphy's law dictates that their failure will occur the moment I become that leader's follower. I also have learned that leadership requires candor. No beating around the bush. True leaders use small words, short sentences, and clear language. Efficient, concise, and honest communication is the hallmark of leadership.

Ed's Final Thoughts

Tom's perspective reflects his experience. As a financial planner his focus is on accumulating wealth for his clients. So, although his reflections relate to success in terms of money, it does not mean that your success needs to be measured that way. I think Tom's insight in this chapter (and in his book as well) goes much deeper than just making money. Like the LM, it reflects that to be successful you must have an awareness of who you are and who you want to be, and develop a plan to become that person. Tom's insight suggests that you cannot be scared of failure and that calculated risk is required to meet bold objectives. As I said earlier, I read Tom's book and found it to be informative, entertaining, and very much aligned with the principles we have discussed. I highly recommend you add his book (*Rich Habits*) to your reading list.

Chapter 9

Are You Ready to Take the Next Step?

Whether you think you can or whether you think you can't, you're right.
- Henry Ford

It is only fitting that I end this book with one of my favorite quotes of all time. I use this quote in some fashion often, particularly when I coach or even just talk to children. It is obvious to me how much their confidence seems to diminish over time. Children generally feel like they can do almost anything up until 8 to 10 years old and then they start to more fully recognize their limitations— often because their limitations have been reinforced many times over by adults. Unfortunately, this recognition comes with reduced confidence and sometimes just an overall inferiority complex. Even worse is that this pattern tends to continue into adulthood. It is too bad because often the only thing holding us back from doing great and spectacular things is ourselves. It is fear of failure and/or ridicule that limits most people from realizing their potential. Within this book, through stories, examples, and guest experts, you have been presented with an opportunity to change yourself. No matter where you are in your life today you can take the next step (seek an opportunity) toward becoming a better leader. Now is the time to act.

As I said at the beginning of this book, I do not claim to have invented the principles presented within this book. The LM is a combination of best practices and principles that I assembled into a framework to organize my thoughts in regards to organizational leadership and management. The LM represents my views based on a wide variety of experiences in the many organizations with which I have been affiliated with in some manner over the last 25 years. I also turned to other accomplished experts in various fields to provide you with a similar but unique perspective on each of the chapter subjects. This book is a result of my passion to continually learn more on the subjects of leadership, management, and teamwork. Now it is up to you to decide what fits and does not fit for you and, more important, to take the bold steps required to take advantage of the opportunities that this book has presented you.

Where do you go from here? I encourage you to take the LM and look at how you can use it to enhance your performance as well as your team's performance in the various COIs to which you belong. The LM is a high-level framework that you can use to optimize team performance and to ultimately become the leader and person you want to become. It is now up to you to fill in the details of who, what, where, when, why, and how you will communicate, plan, execute, monitor, measure, and provide feedback. Of course as you develop and execute your plan you must always consider the people, processes, and technology of the interdependent principles that make up the foundation of the LM. Good luck using the LM to embrace the challenges you will face in advancing yourself as a leader/manager and your organization through strategic thinking, relationship building, and taking advantage of the many opportunities that present themselves to you almost daily.

Armed with an increased awareness of the dynamics described in this book you can become a better leader when you face your life challenges in all your different roles. Remember, we are all leaders! Good luck with your future endeavors and don't forget: no matter how good you are you can always be better.

Finally, I encourage you to share with me success stories as you integrate these principles into your life and develop your own leadership style. You can also go to my website, www.zimmermanconsult.com, to contact me if you or your organization would benefit from a more hands-on, collaborative effort to becoming more efficient and effective. I provide a range of consulting services and seminars that can be adjusted to meet your specific needs. Finally, because I am on a lifetime journey of continual learning on the subject of leadership and personal development, I invite you to pass on to me new ideas or concepts that you have found to be successful in your life as a leader. I hope the material presented in this book provides you with the information and motivation to become the best leader you can be.

Acronyms

AAR – After Action Review
CAC – Common Access Card
CIO – Chief Information Officer
COI – Community of Interest
COP – Community of Practice
COTS – Commercial-off-the-Shelf
CTO – Chief Technology Officer
DOD – Department of Defense
ID – Identification
LM – Leadership Map
KBO – Knowledge-Based Organization
KM – Knowledge Management
KPI – Key Performance Indicators
METL – Mission Essential Task List
PP&T – People, Processes, and Technology
PWC – Principle-Centered Winning
RFP – Request for Proposal
SME – Subject Matter Expert
SOW – Statement of Work
WHCA – White House Communications Agency

Appendix 1

LM Azimuth Check Assessment

Use these questions to capitalize on the key characteristics of people, processes, and technology and guide you through continual improvement inherent within the Leadership Map.

People – Azimuth Check
Trust
What activities occur that provide opportunities to build relationships and trust? Are these recurring events? Are there individuals who routinely do not participate? Why?
Assess the overall environment related to trust by asking team members these questions:
Do you feel the leaders of the organization are trustworthy?
Do you think that the team environment promotes openness and honesty?
Do you sense that issues of trust have been dealt with appropriately?
What character considerations are made during the hiring process?
Are roles and goals used within the organization to help define expectations?
Are character training opportunities provided that can help establish and maintain trust within the organization? What additional activities can be included and why?

People – Azimuth Check

Passion

Assess how passionate the individuals on your team are about their role.

.

Did each individual have input on their roles and the goals?

Do the goals reflect a passion for their role? Would you consider some of the goals to reflect a desire for self improvement?

Do you sense an overall upbeat organizational climate that is normally present with a healthy passion for the organization's mission?

Do you and members of your team also have alternative interests outside of your primary role in this organization? Are there activities designed to promote pursuit of those interests or alternative views and ideas within your primary role with the company? Do these alternatives help to prevent myopic views that can develop from over-zealous focus on any one subject?

People – Azimuth Check

Knowledge and Skill

	Does the organization offer attractive incentives for individuals to seek improvements in knowledge and skill?
	Are there organizational and individual goals associated with continual education?
	Are there organizational and individual incentives and goals related to skill proficiency? Can these incentives tie directly to organizational efficiency and/or effectiveness?
	Does the organization have any type of sponsorship or mentorship program so that less-experienced employees can gain knowledge from more-experienced employees?
	Is there a knowledge-sharing program that allows "best practices" to be shared within the organization? What can be done to improve the sharing of knowledge?

People – Azimuth Check

Complementary

Have the required skills and knowledge been identified and broken down into tasks that support our mission? Have these been captured in our position descriptions?

Do the people we have filling the positions possess the skills and knowledge required?

Do we do a good job of using our personnel performance evaluations and recurring counseling sessions to maintain a focus of the three individual characteristics: trust, passion, and skill/knowledge?

Do you see opportunities to assemble action teams to solve problems that take advantage of the three individual characteristics (trust, passion, and skill/knowledge)?

Does the leadership take advantage of the talents of the individual to create complementary teams? How?

How receptive is leadership to difference of opinion on how to solve problems?

Are there mechanisms and recurring forums in place to allow for team communications that facilitate brainstorming, and consensus on solution for execution?

People – Azimuth Check

Empowerment

	Are individual position roles and goals captured in a manner that assigns responsibility and leadership opportunities?
	Are teams or COPs/COIs created and formalized in some fashion with a mechanism that communicates the team purpose and supporting roles and goals?
	Are "best practice" templates or examples easily accessible to these teams to help them plan and execute the mission at hand?
	What method is in place to review progress and hold the individuals and teams accountable for action? How frequently do these reviews take place?
	Interview employees and discuss their role within these teams. Do they feel that they have been empowered with the authority to get the job done? Do they feel that honest mistakes are written off or that mistakes become the primary focus of the organization's leaders?

Process – Azimuth Check

Simple and Focused

	Is the overall purpose of the process clearly defined?
	Are the steps within the process logical in nature?
	How does each step support the overall intended purpose of the process?
	Are there any steps in which the information required could be obtained automatically from another area?
	During the time since the last review are there any questions or steps that have been repeatedly left out or not performed? Why?
	Have any data or information gaps been identified by anyone involved in the process?

Process – Azimuth Check
Standardized and Repeatable

Is the process being used by different people or groups? How many?

Can the results of the process be measured for efficiency and/or effectiveness? How?

Can each step within the process be measured?

How do the results of the measurements compare to the last review of the process?

Is each person/group using all aspects of the standard process?

Are there differences in performance related to people or teams? If yes, investigate reasons for performance differences.

Process – Azimuth Check
Adaptable

Review the process related to any previous adaptations made during earlier reviews. How do the results compare to previous periods?

Analyze results with appropriate personnel and determine the cause of good and bad performance difference.

Make process changes (if required) based on analysis.

Communicate process performance information and changes based on findings.

Technology – Azimuth Check

Enabling Leaders

What technologies are available for the leader to communicate to his team?

Is the leader comfortable with the technology? Why or why not? What can be done to correct shortfalls?

Are team members comfortable with the technology? Why or why not? What can be done to correct shortfalls?

Is there a communication plan for the organization that identifies what and how the leader will communicate to the team?

Review the communications plan in conjunction with the azimuth check to ensure it is current and relevant. Does the plan align with the organization's mission, vision, and goals?

Technology – Azimuth Check

Enabling Managers

What technologies are used to provide the manager with the information needed to monitor and measure the performance of individuals and teams?

Is the manager comfortable with the technology? Why or why not? What can be done to correct shortfalls?

Are team members comfortable with the technology? Why or why not? What can be done to correct shortfalls?

What recurring reports are used by the manager to analyze performance? List reports and frequency. Identify any information gaps that exist.

Identify any future technology implementations that are already planned. Have the manager's information requirements been identified?

Technology – Azimuth Check

Accelerating Results

Are the intended purposes identified for the different technologies within the organization?

Are there two or more technologies used for the same purpose? Why? Can the organization move to a single technology to accomplish the result?

Are the leaders/managers and staff comfortable with the technology? If not, why and what can be done about it?

Are there established performance objectives outside your organization so that you can benchmark your use of the technology with others in your industry? Capture them and use them to monitor your performance of the technology.

Are there any future technologies that are being implemented? What are the intended purposes? Are there established benchmarks from the old system to baseline the operation for future performance measures?

About the Author

Ed Zimmerman has 25 years of experienced leadership in diverse information systems management and logistics functions that include strategy, policy, operations management, program and acquisition management, lifecycle management, financial management, and human resources management. He earned a reputation as an empowering leader and an action-oriented decision maker known for strategic vision and targeted solutions that solve customers' problems. His approach in analyzing and improving the relationship among people, processes, and technology transforms dysfunctional organizations into highly efficient and productive teams. Mr. Zimmerman provided 20 years service to the United States as an Officer in the Army. His leadership experience in elite military organizations, which includes Delta Force and the White House Communications Agency, contributed to his success as an independent consultant. Mr. Zimmerman has used his operational experience and institutional education to develop his Leadership Map (LM), which he uses to assist leaders and managers in all types of organizations to accomplish their organizational goals.